PASOLI

THE MASSACRE GAME

PASOLINI: THE MASSACRE GAME
Terminal Film, Text, Words 1974-75
Written and edited by Stephen Barber
Translations by Anna Battista
ISBN 9798747925830
Published 2021 by Clash City Sermons
Copyright © Clash City Sermons 2021
All world rights reserved
Genocide was originally published in *Rinascita*, 27th September 1974.
Salò was originally published in *Filmcritica*, August 1975.
We Are All In Danger was originally published in the "Tuttolibri"
supplement of the daily *La Stampa*, 8th November 1975.
Porno-Teo Kolossal was originally published as part of *Pier Paolo
Pasolini: The Dimension Of The Body In Posthumous Scripts* in
Cinema Sessanta, n.5/6, September/December 2002.

INTRODUCTION:
THE MASSACRE GAME

'And we are all guilty, because we are all ready to play the massacre game....'.

This volume focuses on the final year of Pier Paulo Pasolini's life, especially the preoccupations and research that underpinned the shooting of *Salò*, and his intricate responses to the cultural and political impasse experienced in Italy in that year, leading up to 1 November 1975, when Pasolini terminated his last press interview, in which he spoke about 'the massacre game' as a collective process, and, having ignored a final question about how he would 'avoid danger and risk', drove to Rome's Stazione Termini to pick up the hustler Giuseppe Pelosi who – alone, or more likely with a gang of his associates – would murder Pasolini later that night, in the wastelands of Ostia.

As well as a collection of Pasolini's interviews from that last year (including a self-interview conducted on the film-set of *Salò*), this volume also presents the extended medical-legal report synthesised from the investigations into Pasolini's murder, and which reads, in many ways, as a film-treatment authored by Pasolini himself, rather than by Professor Faustino Durante, as though one of the death-inflected fragments of *Salò*'s celluloid had proliferated into a new film, in which the corporeality of Pasolini's past, present and future – so immediately exposed in his anguished final interviews – had been compacted together in an act whose traces now needed to be meticulously analysed and enumerated, through a 'technical report', to reinforce the profound mystery embedded in Pasolini's final gestures. The volume also includes a close analysis of the planned film *Porno-Teo-Kolossal* (the film 'beyond' the terminal film, *Salò*) which Pasolini envisaged shooting at the beginning of 1976, and for which he had prepared a treatment. Like Rainer Werner Fassbinder's planned films to follow his last film *Querelle – I am the Happiness of this World* and *Cocaine*, both annulled by his sudden cocaine-induced death in 1982 – *Porno-Teo-Kolossal* forms a virtual annex to Pasolini's films, with its sparse textual traces demanding their visualisation (into a film with a parallel depth and provocation to *Salò*) by the reader/spectator of the film's residues.

Pasolini's final interviews emanate deep despair and isolation, and the sense that not only his own body, but Italy and the entire world, were about to be engulfed by an amalgam of arbitrary slaughter and maleficent technological consumerism. But at the same time that Pasolini arrives at an erasing impasse, he also films *Salò* and compulsively envisages new projects. Those paradoxes and contradictions – so integral too to Jean Genet's approach to his work – drive both Pasolini's working process and his perception of the wider cultural and political context for his work. Film-making is habitually seen as involving some degree of a collective or collaborative process, but the interview with *Filmcritica* makes clear the utterly rigid solitude and isolation in which Pasolini filmed *Salò* , 'all alone' on the film-set to avoid 'complicity', with his film-crew silently subjugated in their position of intuiting and carrying through his desires. While articulating, in his interviews, a last-ditch renunciation of Italian political culture and its collusions, Pasolini was also planning further active participation in debates at future political conferences.

In the final period of his life, Pasolini travelled extensively outside Italy (to Sweden and France in his last weeks), and moved between his apartment in Rome and his preferred working-place, the 'tower of Chia', a thirteenth-century construction isolated in the rural Viterbo region north of Rome. Beyond Pasolini's own corporeal, public and sexual itinerary, Italy was undergoing acute upheavals in the period on which this volume focuses, thereby intensifying Pasolini's despair and accentuating his creative and vocal responses (just as they inflected the parallel preoccupations of Michelangelo Antonioni, whose film of in-transit journeys through terminal zones and scorched-earth human identities, *The Passenger*, was released in the USA on the same weekend

Mara Cagol.

as Pasolini's death). Political violence and corruption, accelerating urban consumerism and corporate power, and the rise of both left-wing and right-wing terrorism, all marked Pasolini's final year. On 5 June 1975, five months before Pasolini's own death, the left-wing Red Brigade (Brigate Rosse) terrorist movement leader Mara Cagol was trapped and summarily shot dead by police in the Piedmont region of Italy – photographs of her body, fallen on her front, then turned over for facial identification, resonate closely with the police photographs of Pasolini's body on the Ostia wasteland. In the final period of Pasolini's life, the Red Brigade movement was only at an emergent stage and its principal activities would be undertaken later, at the end of the 1970s, after his death; by far the greatest concentration of terrorist activity in Pasolini's final years was instigated by right-wing forces, including the so-called 'strategia della tensione' in which the Italian state was often intimately complicit; the investigating judge Fiorenza Giorgi, analysing the period retrospectively from the 1990s, calculated that between 1969 and 1975 (the year of Pasolini's death), a total of 4,584 terrorist acts were carried out in Italy, with 83% of that total assigned to right-wing perpetrators. It was an era in which political complicity, such as the March 1975 'historical compromise' allying the Italian Communist Party with the Christian Democrats, precipitated the formulation of countercultures and innumerable autonomous acts. Countercultural manifestations took the form of immense music-festivals such as the Festival del Proletariato Giovanile and the rise of influential independent radio stations such as Rome's Radio Onda Rossa, as well as individual gestures of social negation and political refusal; the drug culture of Italy also grew vastly during that era, and in the month following Pasolini's death, new legislation separated the definitions of 'dealer' and 'user' for the first time, with the result that personal users of drugs were no longer subject to legal punishment. And appropriately, for Pasolini's final year, with its dynamics of slaughter, torture, sex and despair, 1975 was a year decreed by the Pope, Paul VI, as a 'Holy Year' of remission and pardon for all sins.

The Massacre Game collects together, for the first time, the essential traces and documents from the extreme experimentation of Pasolini's last year.

I'm very grateful to the film writer Sara Piazza for her guidance with this project, and also to Anna Battista for her expert translations and commitment.

GENOCIDE

A speech made during the Festa de l'Unità, Milan, Summer 1974.

You will excuse some of my terminological inexactitudes or uncertainties. But the origin of the matter – as anticipated – is not literary and, luckily or unluckily, I'm a man of letters, and therefore I do not possess, especially linguistically, the adequate terms to approach it. Let me also make another premilimary remark: what I'm going to say is not the result of a political experience in the literal and professional meaning of this word, but of an almost existential experience.

I will mention straightaway, even though, you may have already understood it, that my thesis is much more pessimistic, and much more bitterly and painfully critical than that of Napolitano[1]. It has as main theme the *genocide*: I do think that the destruction and substitution of certain values in today's Italian society will cause the suppression of large parts of our society even without any mass slaughters and shootings. This is after all not an entirely heretical or heterodox statement.

There is already in Marx's *Manifesto* a part that describes with extremely clear and precise words the genocide as operated by the middle-classes against some parts of the dominated classes, especially the subproletariats and certain colonial populations, rather than just against the workers. Today Italy is living for the first time this phenomenon in a dramatic way: wide strata of population previously cut out of history – the history of middle class domination and revolution – were subjected to this genocide, that is this assimilation to the ways and quality of life of the middle classes.

How does this substitution of values take place? Today this is happening surreptitiously, through a sort of secret persuasion. While during Marx's times it happened through explicit and open violence, colonial conquests and violent impositions, today it happens in subtler, more artful and complex ways, and the process is technically much more mature and profound. New values surreptitiously take the place of old ones, and maybe we don't even need to point it out since the great ideological speeches remain basically unknown to the masses (television, to make an example on which I will come back later on, hasn't certainly divulged Cefis' speech to the students of the Military Academy in Modena)[2].

I will explain myself better by going back to my usual style, that is to that of a man of letters. In these days I'm writing a part of my works in which I tackle this theme in a rather fantastical and metaphorical way: I imagine a sort of descent into Hell during which, to experience the genocide I was talking about, the protagonist walks along the main street of the outskirts of a big town in the South of Italy – probably Rome – and sees a series of visions, each of them corresponding to one of the byroads that leads onto the main one. Each of them is a sort of confusing "bolgia", a Dantesque evil ditch, a hellish circle in the style of the *Divine Comedy*: at the entrance of the street there is a certain model of life surreptitiously put there by the power to which young people, especially children living in that street, quickly adapt to. They have lost their ancient model of life, the one they created by living day by day and about which they were somehow happy, even proud, even though it implied many miseries and had quite a few negative sides – the same ones listed by Napolitano. And now they are trying to imitate the new model surreptitiously established by the ruling class. I'm writing about an entire series of behaviours, roughly fifteen, corresponding to ten circles and five evil ditches, but, to keep it short, I will look only at three of them. I'm underlining once again that the city I'm talking about is a city from the centre-south of Italy and that what I'm going to say is only relatively valid for those people living in Milan, Turin, Bologna etc.

For example, there is the model that, deriving from a certain inter-class hedonism, dictates to the young people who unconsciously imitate it to adapt their behaviour, clothes, shoes, hairstyle and even smile, and the way they act or react, to what they see in the commercial adverts for famous mass produced items, adverts that refer almost racistically to a middle-class lifestyle. The results are obviously pathetic, because a poor youngster from Rome can not keep up to these standards and this causes anxieties and frustrations that bring him to the edge of a serious nevrosis. The opposite model to this one is the model preaching fake tolerance and permissiveness.

In the big cities and in the countryside of the centre-south of Italy there was still a sort of common moral that was rather free, even though it had its own taboos that belonged to it but not to the middle classes; for example it was devoid of any hypocrisy, while it had a sort of shared code of rules to which people used to abide to. At a certain point, power wanted to subject to itself a different kind of person who was first of all a consumer; and a consumer wouldn't have been perfect if he hadn't had a certain sexual permissiveness. Yet young people from the backward regions of Italy tried to abide also to this model in an awkward, pathetic and always nevrotical way. As third and last model we have what I call aphasia, that is the loss of any linguistic skills. The entire centre-south of Italy had its own religious or local traditions linked by a living language, a dialect that was regenerated by continuous inventions; this dialect included a rich vocabulary, full of almost poetical expressions that grew up day after day thanks to the impulse that each and every person added to it. Every evening something new was created – a joke, a witticism, an unexpected word, there was a marvellous linguistic vitality. The ruling class's model blocked people linguistically: in Rome, for example, they are not able to make up things anymore, people fell into a sort of nevrotic aphasia, or they speak in a fake language that does not meet any difficulty nor opposition, almost as if everything was easily speakable – people express themselves as they would in a printed book – or, as an alternative, real aphasia in the clinical sense of the word can be detected. People are incapable of creating metaphors and real linguistic movements, they whimper, push and pull each other or guffaw without being able to say anything.

This is just to give a brief summary of my Hellish vision that, unfortunately, I live in an existential key.

Why is this tragedy taking place in at least two thirds of Italy? Why this genocide caused by the culture surreptitiously imposed by the ruling classes? Because the ruling class totally separated "progress" and "development". The ruling class is only interested in the latter, because it finds profitable only the development. We must make once and for all a dramatic distinction between these two terms, "progress" and "development". It is possible to conceive development without progress, which is something monstrous currently happening in two thirds of Italy; but it is also possible to conceive progress without development, as it would happen in certain rural areas if new models of cultural and civil life were applied without any or with very little material development. What we need – and this in my opinion is the role of the Communist Party and of the progressive intellectuals – is taking conscience of this atrocious disassociation and making the masses aware, so that this disassociation will disappear and development and progress will coincide.

What is instead the type of development that this power wants? If you want to understand it better, read Cefis' speech to the students of the Military Academy in Modena that I mentioned earlier on, and you will find in it a notion about development as multinational – or transnational, as sociologists say – so a power founded on an army that is technologically advanced but, not being national, is completely unrelated to the reality of its own country. All this erases traditional fascism that was founded on nationalism and clericalism, that is founded on old and obviously fake ideals; yet this is actually creating a completely new and even more dangerous form of fascism. I'm going to explain myself better.

As I said, in our country there is a substitution of values and models on which the means of communication, and television in particular, had a great influence. I'm not implying that means of communication have negative connotations per se: in fact I agree that they may be great tools for cultural progress, but, so far, because of the way they were used, they have been, means of an abominable regression, that is of development without progress, of cultural genocide for at least two thirds of Italians. Seen under this light, even the results of the 12th May Referendum[3] are somehow ambiguous. In my opinion, television gave a strong contribution to the "no" votes; in the last twenty years, every kind of religious content was devalued by television. Yes, we often did see the Pope blessing, cardinals opening certain events, we saw processions and funerals, but they were counterproductive facts for the collective religious conscience. In fact what was happening at least on an unconscious level, was a profound process of secularisation that officially handed over the masses of the centre-south of Italy to the power of the *mass media* and, through them, to the real ideology of power: the hedonism of the consumerist power.

For this reason I said – maybe in a rather violent and overexcited way – that the "no" votes have a double soul: on one hand they refer to a real and conscious progress, in which communists and the left wing had a great role; on the other, they are the result of a fake progress, that prompts Italians to accept divorce for the secularisation needs of the bourgeois power, because those ones who accept divorce are good consumers. This is the reason why, for the love of truth and for a painfully critical sense, I can even apocalyptically foresee that, if the part that exercised its power among the "no" votes would prevail, our society would end.

It will not happen because in Italy there is a strong Communist Party and an intelligentsia advanced and progressive enough, yet there is a danger. The current destruction of values does not imply an *immediate* substitution with other values, with their good and bad sides, with the necessary improvement of living standards that they would bring together with a real cultural progress. There is, in between, an imponderable moment in which we are currently living; and here is the great and tragic danger. Think about what a recession may mean in these conditions and you will be shivering if, for an instant, the – maybe arbitrary, maybe fictional – comparison with Germany in the '30s materialises in your mind. There are some analogies between our industrialisation process in the last ten years and the industrialisation process Germany went through in those years: it was in these conditions that consumerism opened the path, after the recession of the 1920s, to Nazism.

Here is the anxiety of a man of my generation who saw the war, the Nazis, the SS and who suffered a trauma never totally overcome.

When I see around me young people losing old popular values and absorbing new models imposed by capitalism, risking in this way to adopt a form of dishumanity, of atrocious aphasia, a brutal absence of critical capacities, a factitious passivity, I recall that these were the typical qualities of the SS and I see the horrid shadow of the hooked cross projecting itself on our own towns. My vision is certainly apocalyptic. But if next to my vision and to the anxiety it produces there wasn't a drop of optimism, namely the thought that the possibility of fighting against all this exists, I wouldn't be here speaking among you.

1. Translator's note: Giorgio Napolitano, 11th President of the Republic of Italy, was in the 1970s the official responsible first for culture and then for the economical policy and the international relations of the Italian Communist Party (PCI, *Partito Comunista Italiano*). Napolitano had spoken earlier on, on the same day as Pasolini's speech, criticising the way the Christian Democrats were leading the country.
2. Translator's note: Pasolini is referring to the speech entitled *La mia patria si chiama multinazionale* ("My home country is called multinational") by the then Eni and Montedison Chairman Eugenio Cefis to the students of the Accademia Militare in Modena in 1972.
3. Translator's note: a referendum on the divorce law was held in Italy on 12th May 1974. Voters were asked if they wanted to repeal a 1970 government law regulating marriage dissolution. Those voting "yes" wanted to outlaw divorce; those voting "no" wanted to keep the law and their right to divorce. The "no" votes prevailed.

SALÒ – AN INTERVIEW

An interview with Pier Paolo Pasolini by Gideon Bachmann and Donata Gallo, August 1975

Filmcritica: You were telling us about a different need in this film, *Salò, or the 120 Days of Sodom*, for what regards the acting, can you tell us more about it?

Pasolini: Yes, in my previous films, I usually instructed professional actors to act like non-professionals, while I would suggest the line they had to deliver to non-professional actors picked from the streets. They would then deliver that line as they wanted, even in their own dialect, and, while editing the film, I would choose the most successful of the improvised lines collected, reiterating them by synchronisation or post-dubbing, and thus ending up with having to use cut-aways to bridge the gaps in continuity. In this film I refuse to use cut-aways; I now insist on exact deliver of the lines so as to create a streamlined, dramatic and already edited structure while I'm shooting the film. Formally I want this film to be like a crystal and not magmatic and chaotic, this is why I'm demanding the best from professional actors and I'm also asking non professionals to act as professionals.

Filmcritica: Does this search for perfection in the acting reflect also on other levels?

Pasolini: Yes it does, in fact all the other elements in this film are much more precise: the movements, the compositions, the make-up – in the past I would do all this with a certain nonchalance, almost with less attention and with more realism, but this would happen because they were more spontaneous, realistic, relaxed and magmatic films! In *Salò* instead everything must be taken care of, even the tiniest details, so for example a death scene is repeated thousands of times until that specific actor playing in it really looks like a man struck dead, and I do not cut a longer scene in shorter fragments since I am conceiving it as a structure serving as a sort of fancy wrapping for the horrible contents, that is de Sade's contribution and that of the fascists. To make sure all these elements work out, I need a structure with a precise and well-determined rhythm that is therefore less realistic because it's more perfect. I gave the film a sort of Dantesque structure – because I think that somehow this is also what de Sade had in mind – dividing the film into days that reflected the theological verticalism of Dante's Hell.

Filmcritica: What do you think about de Sade?

Pasolini: De Sade wasn't the kind of writer who could produce the perfect page every time. Some of his pages are pretty bad in fact, but there are phrases here and there which stand out in extraordinary beauty. Like "All this is good because it is excessive", a lovely phrase. Yet there is one every now and then, since as I said, he couldn't produce the perfect page. If he had cared for the page as a real writer, he would have reached a sort of elegance that he rarely had. He was a writer of structures. Often these were well-controlled, well-designed, elegant like *The 120 Days of Sodom* which has a precise structural base. Other times his structures were endlessly open, flexible like an accordion, with ideas lined up as on a spit.

Filmcritica: Do you feel you have any sense of identification with de Sade? I often think about the disquietude and hurry that you often display while shooting your films, even though in this case it looks like you're controlling it.

Pasolini: Identification? No, because, opposite to de Sade, I was educated and lived in a cultural, literary climate, where form counts, and this is why the page is important to me. I very concretely feel the fact of art. What makes me seem to be in a hurry is the sheer avidity of instantly consuming something that is fascinating me at that precise instant. My other films were devised in a different way: I collected the material to cut later in order to make the film. I had to collect a lot and come home with a full sack to be able to make a rich choice. This time it's different and thus my haste is calculated. First of all, I'm shooting mostly interiors now. I want a formally perfect film. I can't afford to go on collecting magmatically, but I must be more organised during shootings than with the other films.

Filmcritica: Is this the first time you will shoot a film in this way?

Pasolini: No, I already made films like this before, such as *Teorema* ("Theorem") and partly *Porcile* ("Pigsty").

Filmcritica: So in which way does this film fit with the rest of your work?

Pasolini: It represents a new register in which I face the modern world: this is actually the very first time I do it. I did it partly in *Teorema*, but now I'm facing it in all its horror and I think that, for a period of time, this is more or less how I will shoot my films. What's for sure is that I won't do it in a realistic way: I couldn't as I wouldn't be able to physically represent this power that I'm being subjected to. But I could do it as I usually do, using metaphors.

Filmcritica: Are there any precedents in your literary works?

Pasolini: No, maybe the Friulian poems, even though they represent my prehistory. My novels, on the other hand, are magmatic again, within a certain, clear structure. But I always had a tendency to let myself go when things attract me, and I have chapters in my novels which are very much out of proportion, exaggerated speech, for example, and collecting situations, using too many details. The same thing happens in my films, except *Teorema*, *Porcile* and this one. This happened because when I make a film which is basically a metaphor, an allegory, I must work rigidly. Everything you show has a very precise meaning, and you cannot use random choice! In these films there is not space for things that are not functional and significant! So while shooting *Salò* I can't allow myself the luxury of getting lost in a momentary intuition because it makes me smile, and I can't allow myself to fall in love with a landscape, ending up stretching the duration of the film in this way.

Filmcritica: While shooting this film are you somehow repeating the rituality that characterises your previous films?

Pasolini: Yes, this is more or less what I always do in all my films, but in this case I'm taking things to the extreme. The obsessive use of shots and reverse shots, of a close up juxtaposed to another close up, the fact that there are no foreground characters or that there are no characters entering or exiting a specific shot, the lack of sequence shots, are typical elements in all my films, but I would say that in this latest film everything is more crystalline and my habits are taken to a new obsessive level that transforms them.

Filmcritica: What's the common denominator in all your films?

Pasolini: The formal idea of a film, the outline that remains unchanged in all the films and that it is difficult to describe with words. When I decide to shoot a film I do so because I get struck by a formal idea, by a sort of lightning that is actually the synthesis of a film.

Filmcritica: Who's this film for?

Pasolini: It's for everybody. But it's also for another Pasolini, and for all those who can't stand Power for what it does to the human body. Power transforms the latter into an object, it cancels the personality of a human being. This is a film against the anarchy of power, since nothing is more anarchic than power; power arbitrarily does whatever it wants, prompted by its own economical needs that escape common logic. We all hate the power that oppresses us; for example, I particularly hate the current power, that of 1975. It is a power that manipulates human bodies in a horrible way and that can be compared to Hitler's body manipulations. This power manipulates human bodies in the most terrible way, transforming their consciences and instituting new, alienating and fake values, that is the values of consumerism. From this derives what Marx defines as the genocide of living, real and previous cultures. For example, this power destroyed Rome, Romans do not exist anymore, a young Roman man is the shadow of his own self, he is still physically alive, but he finds himself suspended between the ancient values of the Roman popular culture he descends from and the new middle-class values that were imposed upon him.

Filmcritica: What strikes me the most in de Sade is maybe the repetitiousness of the erotic gesture: does this also appear in your film?

Pasolini: Yes, it does. Power reduces everything to a code, to a ritual, also the erotic gestures. The gesticulation of love eternally repeats itself and sodomitic gestures are the most typical of all and the most infertile and useless since they summarise the code of repetitiousness of the sexual act because they are the most gratuitous and the most mechanical of the infinite repetitions of the act of love. It is even worse for the executioner and the torturer because he can undertake his gestures only one single time. For him the problem is one of quantity, because, instead of killing a single, he must kill thousands, in order to be able to repeat his gesture. Or else he must learn to make believe to be killing but not to kill by putting a gun loaded with blanks to the victim's head, pulling the trigger and shooting. The return to life would therefore become a perverse variant since the ritual of death would be by now consumed. This possibility I have used in the film. I have borrowed from both Klossowski and Blanchot the model of God they propose. All these Nietzschean supermen in using the victims' bodies as objects are just another form of Gods on earth. Their model is always God. In negating him they accept his existence.

Filmcritica: You do between two and four takes for one scene, why do you practically avoid rehearsing?

Pasolini: I don't repeat a lot the same scene unless it becomes particularly difficult to obtain what I want. The actors get tired if they repeat a scene a lot of times. In my case I often use nonprofessional actors and they usually give their best straightaway on the first take, thanks to their instinctual understanding of the meaning of a scene. On the other hand, when they repeat a scene a lot of times they lose efficacy as they are not able to bring to perfection their lines, so I instruct them earlier on about how they have to deliver their lines. They say that line for the first time during the first take, and this happens for two main reasons, first because the immediate reality of the film must be shot straightaway, second because you will never be able to foresee which will be the best and most genuine take, but I must admit that often, in the editing room I find myself picking the very first take out of four.

Filmcritica: I visited the set of *Salò* and realised the crew seemed to have a sort of unanimous consensus for your choices, everybody revealed to me they had accepted to work on this film – that is actually too short to gain out of it a consistent financial reward – because your presence actually guaranteed them its success. There was a striking sense of peace, calmness and collaboration on the set, everybody seemed to be very concerned about giving the best they could, and they seemed to be doing so just to make you happy. So when I looked at you all alone thinking by yourself about your film, I wondered, wouldn't it be more desirable to actually collaborate on the film together with the crew?

Pasolini: No, this is a horrible idea as complicity would turn into permissiveness, into paternalism. The person who created the idea for that film and who wanted to shoot it is genuinely interested in it, all the others aren't. I'm happy to hear about the frame of mind of the crew, but that's the best thing that can happen on a film set. For a director being alone is the rule, so I'm not bothered about it. There are already so many problems during a film shoot and, if I started involving other people, they would never be sorted out in a short time. For what regards some technical problems such as the lights, I usually turn to the Director of Photography Tonino Delli Colli, but if I'm unsure about a specific frame I would still have to find a solution by myself and even take the responsibility in case the solution is not efficient enough.

Filmcritica: There are more or less three stages in a film-making proces: 1) the author thinks and writes the film, 2) the shooting, 3) the editing followed by the release. In which of these stages do you feel you're really living the story of your film?

Pasolini: Probably between the first and the second stage, that intermediate phase in which I start looking for the characters I have in mind for my story. The search for the right actor involves me deeply because in that very moment I finally verify if my hypotheses were right, that is to say if a physiognomy I pictured in my mind should have the character I imagine it to have. When I need young carefree, clever, shrewd actors who are still a little bit unsure and awkward, I never look for young people who have just graduated from the actors' academy and who may just be able to badly imitate real people from Rome's *borgate*. I just visit Rome's outskirts and look for those young people who may be able to interpret themselves on the screen. When I need somebody who can act in a more complex part, then I look for professional actors, even though this rarely happens. This remains the most exciting moment for me because the film does not exist yet, but, at the same time, it is taking shape through these characters I'm picking who are often so authentic to inspire me new and interesting scenes for my film.

Filmcritica: You stated that cinema is actually reality seen in an infinite sequence shot, so why do you never use such shots in your films?

Pasolini: Because I make movies and not cinema. It's the same difference between the concepts of "langue" and "parole", that is of language and speech: I use cinema's "parole", therefore its "langue", and my "parole" is made of shots and reverse shots, of close ups juxtaposed to other close ups and so on...

Filmcritica: You shot all your movies by yourself, privileging full figure shots, sometimes using a stand, most of the times just holding the camera, avoiding tracking and aerial shots and other technically advanced effects...

Pasolini: The fact that I'm my own cameraman derives from a very simple reason: while I'm shooting, I'm still searching for something. What I mean is that, since I'm always collecting materials, my act of shooting is another part of my research and not the final interpretation of some shots formally included in the screenplay. It is true that my script often includes not only notes about the characters' movements, but also explanations about the shots, yet they are indicative, I usually decide all the rest once I'm on the set. For what regards my shooting technique, it derives from a precise desire to respect a certain realism. I'm standing for example in front of two young men talking and I put the camera between them and my eyes. By filming them I look at them in the same way I myself or any other person would do in real life. Then I get nearer to imitate via a close up a human being's curiosity, and then I use a selection of shots and reverse shots, to understand how they see each other while they talk. I want their facial expressions to reflect all the action and interpret it, this is essentially what I'm aiming for.

SEX AS A METAPHOR FOR POWER

Pier Paolo Pasolini's "Self-Interview" for Il Corriere della Sera, 25th March 1975

Q. Are the themes in this film somehow anticipated in any of your previous films?

A. Yes, they are. I can mention for example *Porcile* ("Pigsty") and *Orgia* ("Orgy"), a theatre piece that I directed myself (in Turin, in 1968). I conceived it in 1965, wrote it between 1965 and 1968 like *Porcile*, that was also at the time a theatre piece. At the beginning also *Teorema* ("Theorem", released in 1968) was supposed to be a theatrical text. De Sade entered these works via the Theatre of Cruelty, Artaud and, as much as it may sound strange, also via Brecht, an author who, until that moment, I had loved very little and for whom I developed a sudden and overwhelming passion in those years that preceded the student protest. I'm not happy with both *Porcile* and *Orgia*: estrangement and detachment are not for me, in the same way as "cruelty" is not for me.

ON CRUELTY

Q. So what about *Salò*?

A. Yes, it's true, *Salò* will be a cruel film, so cruel that (I imagine) I will have to distance myself from it, pretending not to believe in it or to be toying around with this idea a little bit in a frightening way... But let me finish my feedback about the links with my previous films. In 1970 I was in the Loire Valley. I was scouting for locations for *Il Decameron* ("The Decameron") and I was invited to a debate with the students of the

University of Tours. Franco Cagnetta teaches there and he gave me a book about Gilles de Rais and the documents about his trial, thinking that I may have found them inspirational for one of my films. I seriously thought about this possibility for quite a few weeks (a beautiful biography of Gilles de Rais, edited by Ernesto Ferrera, was recently published in Italy). Then I decided not to do it. I was taken too much by my *Trilogy of Life*...

Q. Why did you decide not to do it?
A. Because it was meant to be a "cruel" film and a cruel film would have been political and (revolutionary and anarchic in that precise moment of time) and therefore insincere. Maybe I prophetically thought that the most sincere thing I could have done in that precise moment of time was to shoot a film in which sex was a sort of compensation for repression, something that wasn't happening anymore. Indeed, in quite a short span of time, tolerance turned sex into something sad and obsessive. I evoked in the *Trilogy of Life* the ghosts of the characters from my previous realistic films. I did it with no will to denounce, but with such a violent love for the "long-lost times" that it turned into a denunciation not of a particular human condition, but of the (perforce permissive) present times we are living in. We irreversively live in these present times, we have adapted to them. Our memory is always bad; we are therefore living immersed in the current repression of the tolerant power – the most horrid of all kinds of repressions. There is no happiness in sex anymore. Young people are ugly or desperate, bad or defeated.

Q. Is this what you are trying to express in *Salò*?
A. I don't know. This is certainly its "background". I can't ignore it. It reflects the mood I'm in. It's what I have in my thoughts and what I personally suffer in my heart. Therefore, this is maybe what I want to express in *Salò*. A sexual relationship is a language (this was clear and explicit in my work such as *Theorem*): languages or systems of signs are currently changing. The language or system of signs regarding sex radically changed in Italy in just a few years. I can't cut myself outside the evolution of any linguistic convention in my society, including the

sexual one. Today sex is the satisfaction of a social obligation, not a pleasure that goes against social obligations. From this derives a sexual behaviour radically different from the one I was used to and for me this trauma was (and still is) almost intolerable.

Q. In a nutshell, for what regards sex in *Salò*...
A. Sex in *Salò* is a representation of – or a metaphor for – this situation we are living in at the moment: sex as obligation and ugliness.

Q. But you also have other intentions that are maybe less deep and more direct...
A. Yes, I do and I would like to talk about these ones now. Apart from a metaphor for the (compulsory and ugly) sexual intercourse that the tolerance of consumerist power is obliging us to live in these years, sex in *Salò* (and there is a lot of it) is also a metaphor for the relationship of power with those ones who are subjected to it. In other words it is the representation (maybe the dreamy representation) of what Marx calls the commodification of man, the reduction of the human body to a thing (through its exploitation). Therefore sex has a horrible metaphoric role in my film. It's completely the opposite of what it was in the *Trilogy of Life* (if we consider how, in repressive societies, sex was also an innocent derision of power).

Q. Yet aren't your *120 Days of Sodom* taking place in Salò in 1944?
A. Yes, they are, in Salò and in Marzabotto. I took fascist power – and in particular the power of the fascists from the Salò Republic – as a symbol of that power that transforms people into objects (as it happens for example in the best Miklos Jankso films). But, as I said, it is a symbol. That archaic power facilitates my representation. I actually leave to all the film a sort of wide margin that dilates that archaic power taken as a symbol of each and every form of imaginable of power... And then... This is what I mean: power is anarchic. And power has never been more anarchic as it was during the Salò Republic.

Q. What has de Sade got to do with it?

A. A lot because de Sade was the great poet of the anarchy of power.

Q. In which way?

A. There is always something wild in power – in any kind of power, be it legislative or executive. In the theory and the practice of power we establish and apply the most primeval and blind form of violence of the strong against the weak ones, that is of the exploiters upon the exploited. The anarchy of the exploited ones is desperate, idyllic and, above all, completely airy-fairy and eternally destined to remain unfulfilled. The anarchy of power based on codes of theory and practice: the powerful characters in de Sade write the rules and regularly apply them.

THREE CIRCLES

Q. You will excuse me if I go back to the more practical aspects, but in which way does all this come together in the film?

A. It's simple and, more or less, it happens in the same way as in de Sade's book: four ontological and therefore arbitrary powerful men (a Duke, a Banker, a Magistrate and a Bishop), "reduce to things" a group of humble victims. They do so in a sort of sacred representation that, following what were probably the original intentions of de Sade, is formally structured in the style of Dante's *Divine Comedy*, so an Ante-Hell and three Circles. The main (metonimical) figure of speech employed is the accumulation (of crimes), but also the hyperbole, and in the film I would also like to push myself to the limits of the audiences' tolerability.

Q. Who are the actors starring as the four monsters?

A. I'm not sure they will be monstrous. But they won't be any more or less monstrous than the victims. When I picked the actors I tried to mix them as usual: I chose a generic actor who in more than 20 years of work never pronounced one single line, Aldo Valletti; an old friend of mine from Rome's *borgate* (I met him at the time of *Accattone!*) Giorgio Cataldi; a writer, Uberto Paolo Quintavalle, and, last but not least, Paolo

Bonacelli, an actor.

Q. And who will star in the role of the storytelling "witches"?
A. Three beautiful women (the fourth woman in my film is a pianist, because the circles are actually three): Hélène Surgère, Caterina Boratto and Elsa de'Giorgi. The pianist is Sonia Saviange. I chose the two French actresses after seeing in Venice the film *Femmes Femmes* directed by Vecchiali: it's a beautiful film in which the two actresses, to remain in the linguistic context of their native tongue, play their roles in a really sublime way.

Q. Who will be the victims?
A. Amateur boys and girls (at least some of them: the girls were picked among fashion models because they had to have nice bodies and because – above all – they didn't have to be afraid of showing them).

Q. Where will you be shooting?
A. In Salò (outdooor scenes), in Mantua (indoor scenes and the outdoor scenes showing the kidnappings and the searches), in Bologna and in the surrounding areas: the village on the Reno river will be used as the destroyed Marzabotto...

Q. I know that the shooting started two weeks ago. Can you tell us something about your work on the set?
A. Please, spare me this question. There is nothing more sentimental than a director talking about his work on his own set.

SALÒ – NOTES

Notes written by Pasolini and published in an Italian English-language press book for **Salò**.

FOREWORD

This film is a cinematographic transposition of Sade's novel *The 120 Days of Sodom*. I should like to say that I have been absolutely faithful to the psychology of the characters and their actions, and that I have added nothing of my own. Even the structure of the story line is identical, although obviously it is very synthesised. To make this synthesis I resorted to an idea Sade certainly had in mind – Dante's Inferno. I was thus able to reduce in a Dantesque way certain deeds, certain speeches, certain days from the whole immense catalogue of Sade. There is a kind of 'Anti-Inferno' (the Antechamber of Hell) followed by three infernal 'Circles': 'The Circle of Madness'; 'The Circle of Shit', and 'The Circle of Blood'. Consequently, the Story-Tellers who, in Sade's novel, are four, are three in my film, the fourth having become a virtuoso – she accompanies the tales of the three others on the piano.

Despite my absolute fidelity to Sade's text, I have however introduced an absolutely new element: the action instead of taking place in eighteenth-century France, takes place practically in our own time, in Salò, around 1944, to be exact.

This means that the entire film with its unheard-of atrocities which are almost unmentionable, is presented as an immense sadistic metaphor of what was the Nazi-Fascist 'dissociation' from its 'crimes against humanity'. Curval, Blangis, Durcet, the Bishop – Sade's characters (who are clearly SS men in civilian dress) behave exactly with their victims as the Nazi-Fascists did with theirs. They considered them as objects and destroyed automatically all possibility of human relationship with them.

This does not mean that I make all that explicit in the film. No, I repeat again, I have not added a single word to what the characters in Sade have to say nor have I added a single detail to the acts they commit. The only points of reference to the 20th century are the way they dress, comport themselves, and the houses in which they live.

Naturally there is some disproportion between the four protagonists of Sade turned into Nazi-Fascists and actual Nazi-Fascists who are historically true. There are differences in psychology and ideology. Differences and also some incoherence. But this accentuates the visionary mood, the unreal nightmare quality of the film. This film is a mad dream, which does not explain what happened in the world during the 40s. A dream which is all the more logical in its whole when it's the least in its details.

SALÒ AND SADE

Practical reason says that during the Republic of Salò it would have been particularly easy given the atmosphere to organise, as Sade's protagonists did, a huge orgy in a villa guarded by SS men. Sade says explicitly in a phrase, less famous than so many others, that nothing is more profoundly anarchic than power – any power. To my knowledge there has never been in Europe any power as anarchic as that of the Republic of Salò: it was the most petty excess functioning as government. What applies to all power was especially clear in this one.

In addition to being anarchic what best characterises power – any power – is its natural capacity to turn human bodies into objects. Nazi-Fascist repression excelled in this.

Another link with Sade's work is the acceptance/non-acceptance of the philosophy and culture of the period. Just as Sade's protagonists accepted the method – at least mental or linguistic – of the philosophy of the Enlightened Age without accepting all the reality which produced it, so do those of the Fascist Republic accept Fascist ideology beyond all reality. Their language is in fact their comportment (exactly like the Sade protagonists) and the language of their comportment obeys rules which are much more complex and profound than those of an ideology. The vocabulary of torture has only a formal relation with the ideological reasons which drive men to torture. Nonetheless with the characters in my film, although what counts is their sub-verbal language, their words also have a great importance. Besides their verbiage is rather wordy. But such wordy verbiage is important in two senses: firstly it is part of the presentation, being a 'text' of Sade's, that is being what the characters think of themselves and what they do; and, secondly, it is part of the ideology of the film, given that the characters who quote anachronistically Klossowski and Blanchot are also called upon to give the message I have established and organised for this film: anarchy of power, inexistence of history, circularity (non-psychological not even in the psychoanalytic sense) between executioners and victims, an institution anterior to a reality which can only be economic (the rest, that is, the superstructure, being a dream or a nightmare).

IDEOLOGY AND MEANING OF THE FILM

We should not confuse ideology with message, nor message with meaning. The message belongs in part – that of logic – to ideology, and in the other part – that of irreason – to meaning. The logical message is almost always evil, lying, hypocritical even when very sincere. Who could doubt my sincerity when I say that the message of *Salò* is the denunciation of the anarchy of power and the inexistence of history? Nonetheless put this way such a message is evil, lying, hypocritical, that is logical in the sense of that same logic which finds that power is not at all anarchic and which believes that history does exist. The part of the message which belongs to the meaning of the film is immensely more real because it also includes all that the author does not know, that is, the boundlessness of his own social, historical restrictions. But such a message can't be delivered. It can only be left to silence and to the text. What finally now is the meaning of a work? It is its form. The message therefore is formalistic; and precisely for that reason, loaded infinitely with all possible content provided it is coherent – in the structural sense.

STYLISTIC ELEMENTS IN THE FILM

Accumulation of daily characteristics of wealthy bourgeois life, all very proper and correct (double-breasted suits, sequinned, deep cut gowns with dignified white fox furs, polished floors, sedately set tables, collections of paintings, in part those of 'degenerate' artists (some futuristic, some formalistic); ordinary speech, bureaucratic, precise to the point of self caricature.

'Veiled' reconstruction of Nazi ceremonial ways (its nudity, its military simplicity at the same time decadent, its ostentations and icy vitality, its discipline functioning like an artificial harmony between authority and obedience, etc).

Obsessive accumulation to the point of excess of sadistic ritualistic and organised deeds; sometimes also given a brutal, spontaneous character.

Ironic corrective to all this through a humour which may explode suddenly in details of a sinister and admittedly comic nature. Thanks to which suddenly everything vacillates and is presented as not true and not crude, exactly because of the theatrical satanism of self-awareness itself. It is in this sense that the direction will be expressed in the editing. It is there that will be produced the mix between the serious and the impossibility of being serious, between a sinister, bloody Thanatos and curate Bauba.

In every shot it can be said I set myself the problem of driving the spectator to feeling intolerant and immediately afterwards relieving him of that feeling.

SALÒ – A PHOTO GALLERY

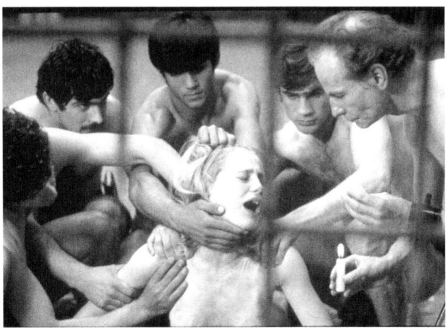

34

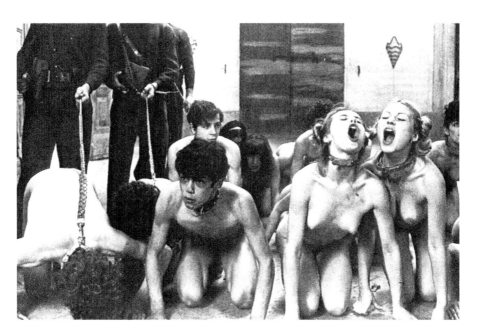

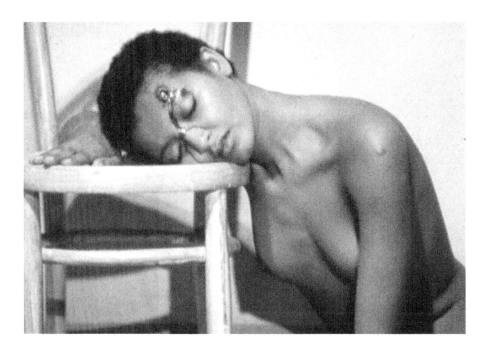

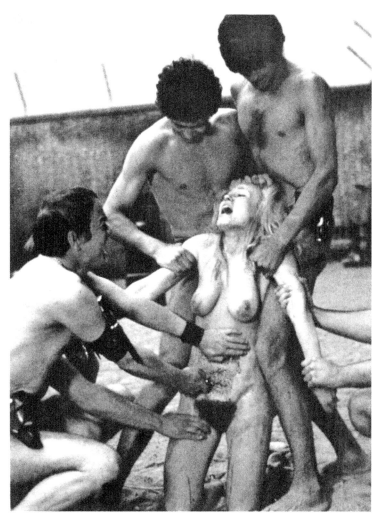

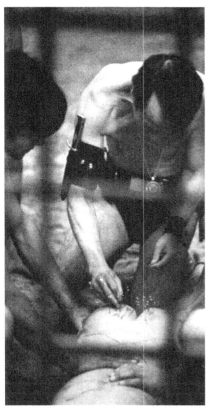

40

41

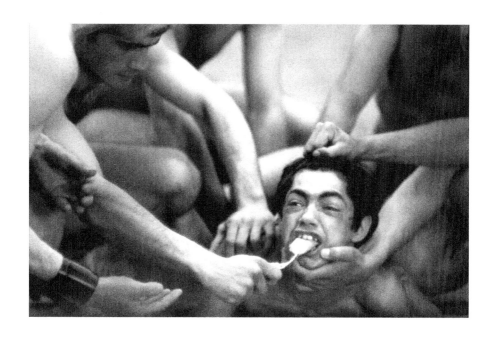

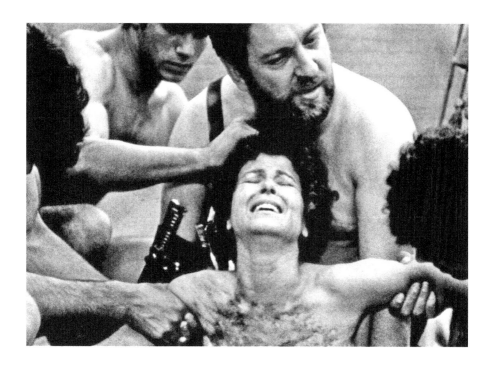

45

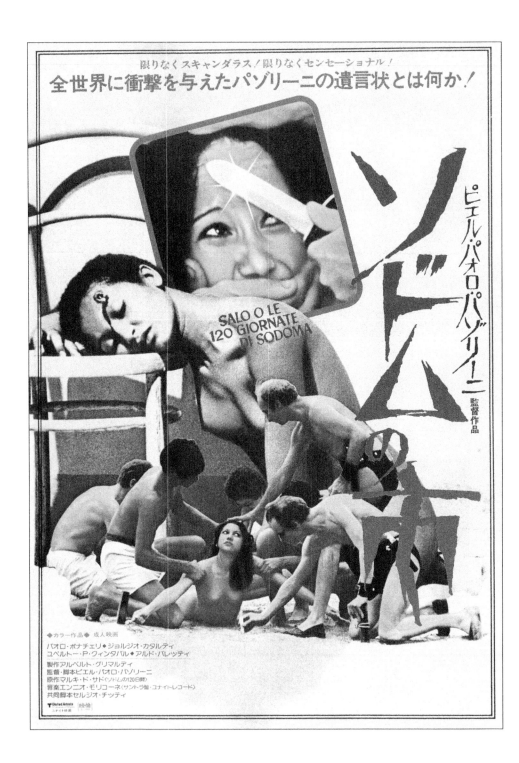

WE ARE ALL IN DANGER

Pier Paolo Pasolini Interviewed by Furio Colombo, 1st November 1975

Pasolini, in your articles and writings you provided us with different definitions to describe the things you hate. You started a fight, by yourself, against a lot of things – institutions, beliefs, people, powers. To facilitate our interview, I will simply say "the situation" and you will know that I intend to talk about what you are fighting against. So my first point is the following objection: the "situation" with all the bad things that it implies, basically allows you to be who you are, Pasolini. What I mean is, you have the talent and the merit for saying specific things, but what about the topics? The topics are basically offered to you by this "situation", so the publishing or the film industry, the political situation or even simple objects. Let's pretend that you had a magic touch, and you had the power of saying something and of making disappear all the things you hate. Wouldn't you end up alone with no topics to tackle anymore, with no topics to fight against, I mean…

Yes, I do understand what you mean. Well, I'm not just trying to pretend I do have that magic touch, but I do believe I have it and not in a mediumistic sense. Because I do know that harping on the same subject can eventually demolish it. The exponents of the Radical Party provide us with a little example: they are just very few people but they shook the conscience of an entire country (and you know perfectly well that I often do not agree with them, but at the moment I'm getting ready to go to their convention). History provides us with more famous examples: refusal has always been a very important act carried out by saints, and hermits but also by intellectuals. The very few people who made history are those ones who said no, not the courtesans and the cardinals' assistants. Therefore, an act of refusal must be total and not partial, in a nutshell it must not focus on this or that nor must it be dictated by wisdom. My dear friend, Eichmann was very wise, but what did he lack? He didn't know how to say no at the very beginning, when the only thing he dealt with was the ordinary administration, the bureaucracy. Maybe he told his friends, I do not like Himmler that much. He may have muttered and grumbled, as you do in a publishing house, in the office of a newspaper, among the people forming the *sottogoverno* (sub-government) or on television. Maybe he objected because this or that train stopped once a day to allow the people who were being deported to go to the toilet or to have some bread and water, when two stops along the line would have been cheaper and more practical. Yet he never tried to stop the machine of power. So there are three points to take into consideration here: what is "the situation", as you call it, why you should stop it or destroy it and in which way (...)

In your opinion, what is power, where is it, where does it live and in which ways do you take it out into the light?

Power is an educational system that divides us into those who subjugate and those who are subjugated. But be very careful: that same educational system forms all of us, from the people in the so-called establishment to the poorest social classes. This is the main reason why we all want the same things and behave in the same ways. Members of the establishment may use a board of directors or a stock exchange manoeuvre; people from more disadvantaged classes may use a metal bar. You essentially use a metal bar to violently obtain what you want. But why do you want it? Because they told you that wanting something is a virtue and you are therefore exercising your right-virtue. So you're a murderer, but you're essentially good.

They said you are not able to distinguish between politics and ideology anymore, that you are not able to detect the profound difference between those among the young people who are fascists

and those who aren't fascists.

This is actually the reason why earlier on I mentioned to you the railway timetable. Have you ever seen those puppets that make kids laugh because their body faces one direction and their heads another? I think that Totò[1] managed to recreate such a trick. Well, this is how I see all those intellectuals, sociologists, experts and journalists full of their noble intentions: with their body here and their minds somewhere else. I'm not saying there is no fascism. I'm just saying stop talking about going to the beach if we're on the mountains since we are dealing with a different kind of landscape here. There is a sort of desire to kill here and this desire binds us like sinister brothers in the sinister failure of an entire social system. I guess it would be easier to isolate the black sheep. I do see the black sheep. In fact there are quite a few ones around and I can see all of them. As I told Moravia, this is the problem: I'm paying a price for the life I lead…It's as if I were descending into Hell. Back from my journey – if I ever came back – I would have experienced other things, more things than other people. I'm not saying that you would have to believe what I recounted to you after my journey, but you would have to keep on changing topic to avoid facing the truth.

But what is the truth?

I'm sorry I've used this word. I wanted to say "evidence". But let me put some order into things. The first tragedy we live is one shared, compulsory and wrong education that pushes us to own everything at any price. We are pushed and pulled around like a strange dark army, some of us fight with the heavy artillery, others with just a metal bar. As it usually happens, the group gets divided and some decide to fight with the weak ones. But I think that, in one way or the other, we are all weak because we are all victims. And we are all guilty, because we are all ready to play the massacre game, as long as we are able to own everything at the end of the slaughter. In a nutshell, the education we received can be summarised with these words – having, owning and destroying.

But let me go back to my first question. You magically abolish

everything, but your job is writing books and you need people who read them. Therefore you need educated consumers for your intellectual products. You make films and therefore you need not only a large audience (in fact you often manage to achieve popular success, so you are avidly "consumed" by your audience), but you also need a great technical, organisational, industrial machine in between. If you make all this disappear with a sort of early Catholic or early Chinese magic monasticism, what will you be left with?

I will be left with everything. Indeed, I will be left with myself; I'm alive, I'm in this world, I can see, I can work, I can understand. There are hundreds of ways to tell stories, to listen to languages, reproduce dialects and create a puppet theatre. The others will be left with much more. They, educated or ignorant like myself, will be able to stand up to me. The world will become a larger place, everything will be ours and we won't need the Stock Exchange, the Board of Directors or the metal bar to steal from each other. You see, in the world that many of us dreamt about (I'm repeating it to you: read last year's railway timetable or read the timetable of many years ago) there was the evil master with the top hat and the pockets full of dollars and the emaciated widow with her children, asking for justice. In a nutshell, Brecht's beautiful world.

And you miss that world.

No! I miss the poor and genuine people who fought to abolish that master without turning into him. Since they were excluded from everything, nobody had managed to colonise them. I'm scared of these slaves in revolt because they behave exactly like their plunderers, desiring everything and wanting everything at any price. This dark obstination leading to total violence is not letting us see who we are. Whoever is taken dying to the hospital is more interested – if there is still some life left in them – in hearing what the doctors will tell them about their chances to live, than in what the police will tell them about the dynamics of the attempted murder perpetrated against them. I'm not putting intentions on trial and I'm not interested in the cause-effect chain, or in spotting who did this or that first and who is the guilty head of the gang. I think we have defined what you call "the situation". It is a bit like when it rains and the manhole covers are blocked: the innocent rain water rises and, even though it doesn't have the fury of the sea or the rage of a river, for a very simple reason, it doesn't go down, but rises. It is the same rain water that appeared in so many children's poems and songs about "singing in the rain". Yet it rises and drowns you. If we have reached this point I would like to add let's not waste time to label things, but let's see how we can let water drain away before we drown.

So, for this reason, you would like all people to be ignorant and happy shepherds with no compulsory education.

It sounds very stupid putting things like this. But compulsory education creates by force desperate gladiators. Like desperation or rage, the crowd gets bigger. So let's say I made a provocation (even though I don't think I did). But tell me another thing: it's obvious that I regret the genuine and direct revolution of the oppressed masses whose main aim is freeing themselves to become their own masters. My best thoughts may even inspire me one of my next poems, but, surely, what I know and what I'm seeing at the moment will not inspire me. What I mean is, I go down to Hell and I discover things that do not bother other people. But be careful: Hell is rising and it's coming at you. It is true that it dreams its uniform and (sometimes) its justification, but it's also true that its desire of hitting with a metal bar, of attacking, of killing is strong and random. And this won't remain for a long time the private and risky experience of those ones who have "experienced violence". Do not delude yourself. Together with school, television, and the calmness of your newspapers, you are the great preservers of this horrid order based upon the idea of owning and destroying. Blessed are thou who are happy when you can put on a murder a label. This looks to me like another of the many mass culture operations. Since one cannot stop certain things from happening, one finds peace in pretence.

But abolishing surely means to create as well, if you don't consider

yourself a destroyer. Your books, for example, what's their final aim? I don't want to become like those ones who get anxious more about culture than about people, but these people that you save can't behave like primitives anymore (this is an accusation that is frequently moved against you) in your vision of a new world and, if we do not want to use the "most advanced" forms of repression…

Which makes me shiver.

If we do not want to use commonplace definitions, we must still give out some indications. For example, in sci-fi, like in Nazism, books are often burnt as a sign of initial extermination. If we close schools and we close television stations, how will you keep your vision alive?

I think I have already explained myself with Moravia. To "close down" in my language means to change. And we must dramatically and drastically change things to reflect the dramatic and drastic situation we are living in. What is not allowing me to have a real debate with Moravia and above all with Firpo[2], for example, is that we seem not to be able to see the same scene happening around us, or not to know the same people or not to hear the same voices. You as a journalist may think that something happens only when it appears written down and titled on the pages of a newspaper. But what's behind this piece of news? I think we are missing the surgeon analysing the fact and then stating: ladies and gentlemen, this is not cancer, it's just a little piece of news. What is cancer? It's something that changes all the cells, that makes them grow at a crazy rhythm, without respecting any previously established logic. So, is the ill person who dreams about his previous health a nostalgic, even though before the illness struck he was a stupid and a wretch? So, first of all, we will have to make an effort to have the same vision. I listen to the politicians – all the politicians – with all their little presumptions and I turn into a madman as they prove they do not know which country they are talking about, they are as far away as the moon. And together with them there are the men of letters, the sociologists and the experts in any kind of fields.

So why do you think that for you some things are clearer?

I don't want to talk anymore about myself, maybe I have already said too much. Everybody knows that, as a person, I do pay for what I say. But there are also my books and my films that end up paying for me. Maybe I'm wrong after all, but I keep on thinking that we are all in danger.

Pasolini, if you see life in this way – and I don't even know if you will accept this question – how do you think you will avoid danger and risk?

It was late and Pasolini hadn't turned on the light, so it became difficult to take notes. We leafed through my notes. Then he asked me to leave my questions with him. "There are some bits that sound a bit too definite. Let me think about them, let me go through them and let me think about a conclusion. I do have something in mind to reply to your question. I find it easier to write than to speak. I will give you back the notes I'm adding tomorrow morning". The day after, on a Sunday, the lifeless body of Pier Paolo Pasolini was in the morgue at Rome's police headquarters.

1 Translator's note: Antonio De Curtis, better known by his stage name Totò, was an Italian comedian, film and theatre actor, writer, singer and songwriter. The heir of the Commedia dell'Arte tradition, he was famous for mimicking the body movements of a puppet in some of his performances. He also starred in some of Pier Paolo Pasolini's fims such as *Uccellacci e Uccellini* ("The Hawks and the Sparrows", 1966).
2 Translator's note: Alberto Moravia (1907-1990) was an Italian writer; Luigi Firpo (1915-1989) was an Italian historian and politician.

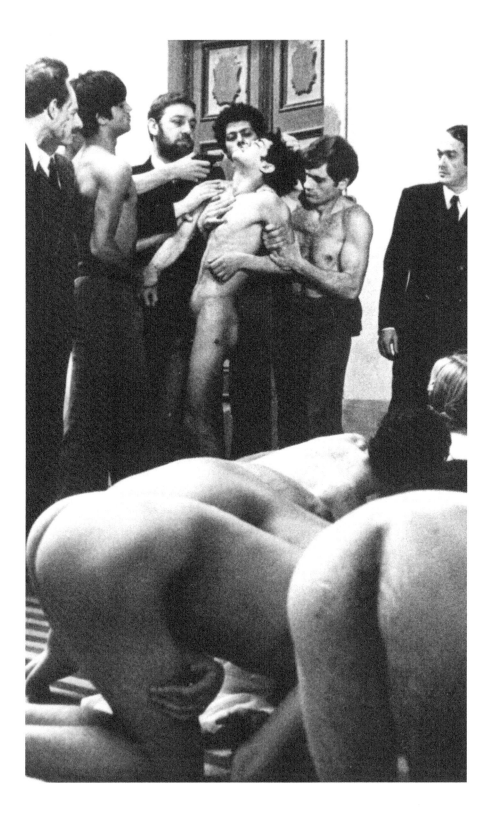

PASOLINI AND SADE: A MALEFICENT OBSESSION

An essay by Stephen Barber

1.
ANTE-INFERNO

Salò is the unique space where film terminally collides with death.

'Death does determine life, I feel that, and I've written it, too, in one of my recent essays, where I compare death to film-montage. Once life is finished, it acquires a sense; up to that point it has not got a sense; its sense is suspended and therefore ambiguous... For me, death is the maximum of epicness and myth.'[1]
　　–Pier Paulo Pasolini, 1968

2.
CIRCLE OF OBSESSIONS

During the production in 1975 of what would be his ultimate film, *Salò* – adapted from Sade's novel *120 Days of Sodom* and transposed to the final moments of the fascist dictatorship in mid-1940s Italy – the film-maker and poet Pier Paulo Pasolini often asserted that he wanted that film to be 'the last movie'[2]: not only his own last movie, but also that of the entire human species: a film of terminal images, before the processes of cultural and social erasure which Pasolini incessantly denounced had engulfed and nullified the visual image entirely. The images of *Salò* –

revelatory of the structures of cruelty and of the sexual origins of human atrocities and massacres – would then form a kind of malign legacy, left for any non-human species which, at some point in the future, might want to look back upon the memories and obsessions of the human species. The concept of the 'last film' was one that attracted many other film-makers during the era of tumultuous upheaval, revolutionary terrorism and worldwide violence that extended from the mid-1960s to the late-1970s; in the USA, the actor-director Dennis Hopper had already adopted that notion of a 'last movie' for the film-title of his seminal, drug-disintegrated masterwork of 1971. However, *Salò* was not the first Pasolini film to be conceived of as a terminal exercise; like his contemporary, the West German director Rainer Werner Fassbinder, Pasolini was perpetually announcing his abandonment of film-making, while simultaneously planning another film-project that would push beyond the extreme limit of his current film. Similarly, the novelist Jean Genet – a profound source of inspiration for Pasolini – declared in *The Thief's Journal* (1949) that it would be his last novel, then asserted in that novel's final two sentences that it would, after all, have a sequel (which never actually transpired). For Pasolini, that film beyond-the-end was to have been a project entitled *Porno-Teo-Kolossal*, which was in preparation to be shot, in New York, Naples and Paris, in the first months of 1976, based on a 75-page film-treatment largely composed of dialogue. However, whether by chance or intention, *Salò* would mark the very end of Pasolini's work – shortly after he had finished editing it, he was savagely murdered by a boy-hustler whose penis he had been sucking only minutes earlier.

Salò was a terminal aberration in Pasolini's work. Unusually, he took on a project which he had not developed himself; his collaborator Sergio Citti had initiated the project, intending to direct it himself, but could not find a producer for it. Pasolini had no difficulty in attracting the producer Alberto Grimaldi, who had had an immense success with *Last Tango in Paris*, directed three years earlier by Bernardo Bertolucci. Once Pasolini had taken on the project, at the beginning of 1975, he researched it intensively; alongside Sade's own work, he read essays on Sade by Georges Bataille (notably, Bataille's preface to Sade's book), Roland Barthes, Pierre Klossowski and Maurice Blanchot, as well as conducting research into the last phase of Italian fascism. And in August 1975, following the film's shooting-period, he would meet with the Surrealist artist Man Ray, who had painted an 'imaginary portrait' of Sade in 1938; Pasolini was contemplating using the portrait on posters for his film.

The Marquis de Sade's *120 Days of Sodom* details the acts of four atheistic Parisian 'libertines' who possess the wealth and power to realize a plan to have sixteen aristocratic young boys and girls kidnapped from their homes, and brought to an isolated castle in Switzerland, the Castle of Silling; accompanied by four story-tellers and eight well-endowed 'cockmongers', the libertines spend four months inflicting an escalating series of sexual tortures on the boys and girls, before finally slaughtering them and returning to Paris. The boys and girls to be massacred are all selected for their exceptional beauty (especially that of their rear-ends), for their young age (between twelve and fifteen), and for their social origins: Augustine, for example, is described by Sade as 'fifteen years old; daughter of a Languedoc baron, with an alert and pretty face'[3]. Sade completed his account of the first of the four months, November, while imprisoned for acts of debauchery at the Bastille prison in Paris in 1785. However, the remaining three parts of the book (for the months of December to February) were only written in the form of notational drafts: skeletal enumerations of the acts undertaken by the libertines, and cryptic summaries of the accompanying story-tellers' narratives. It appears that Sade intended to publish the first part of the book separately, and then to complete each of the three other parts as the publication progressed; however, the manuscript, written on a long scroll of paper, was lost during the revolutionary riots of 1789, and only re-discovered in the early twentieth century. The French Revolution changed Sade's fortunes: released from the Bastille, he initially became a revolutionary judge (though a lenient one, who rarely condemned anyone brought before him), but then fell into poverty and ended his life in the benign incarceration of the Charenton asylum-hospital, on the edge of Paris.

Pasolini moved the action of the novel in time, to the period 1944-

45, thirty years prior to the moment of the film's making. He also moved the action geographically, from an impregnable, mountain-top castle in Switzerland to a salubrious lake-side villa in the small resort town of Salò, overlooking a bay on the Riviera Bresciana, on the banks of Lake Garda in northern Italy. It was in Salò that the Italian fascist dictator Benito Mussolini (who had held power since the year of Pasolini's birth, 1922) established his short-lived 'Republic of Salò' with his remaining supporters. Although Mussolini does not appear as a character in Pasolini's film, his desperate, extreme situation of that period is omnipresent; his 'Republic of Salò' was a final pocket of fascism, ready to defend itself at all costs, by acts of atrocity, after the Italian government had concluded a surrender with the British and American forces, thereby changing sides in the last phase of the Second World War. The Italian government had then deposed and imprisoned Mussolini in 1943, confining him to a hotel on the inaccessible peak of the Gran Sasso mountain in the Abruzzo region, east of Rome, expecting to be able to try him at the end of the war; but Mussolini's friend and ally, Adolf Hitler, was determined to rescue Mussolini from Gran Sasso, and dispatched his best pilot to land on the mountain-peak and spirit Mussolini away to the Lake Garda region, which was still held by the German forces. Mussolini was then installed as the dictator of the northern part of Italy still under the control of the Germans, while the invading British and American forces were rapidly advancing northwards through Italy, after landing in Sicily. As that advance reached the north, Mussolini's chaotic 'Republic of Salò' quickly disintegrated; on the run from partisans, he was captured and cursorily machine-gunned to death in April 1945, in a village alongside Lake Como, then hung upside-down, alongside his mistress, in the Piazzale Loreto in Milan. News of the ignominy of Mussolini's killing led Hitler to commit suicide, in order to avoid meeting a similar fate, as Josef Stalin's Soviet army closed-in on Hitler's own headquarters in Berlin.

Pasolini knew the Salò region of Lake Garda well, and had lived for a time in that area in his youth (his father was a professional soldier: in fact, a professional fascist, and the father's military postings had meant that the Pasolini family had moved constantly from one region of northern Italy to another, during Pasolini's youth). Pasolini also had intimate personal knowledge of the atrocities committed by the Italian fascists on the civilian population during the final stages of the conflict; he had witnessed the aftermath of acts of mass execution. In an interview about his film's location in space and time, he said: 'It was an epoch of sheer cruelty, searches, executions, deserted villages, all totally useless, and I suffered a great deal.'[4] During the period in which *Salò* is set, Pasolini's only brother, Guido, was executed at the age of twenty, in March 1945, in the course of his anti-fascist guerrilla activities, first wounded and captured along with his group of partisans, then coldly finished-off with a bullet in the head; after the war was over, Pasolini learned that his brother had died uselessly – he had not been killed by the Nazis or Italian fascists after all, but instead had been executed as the result of a chaotic squabble between two rival anti-fascist partisan groups.

In writing the film-script for *Salò*, Pasolini made a number of significant changes in the characters of Sade's novel; in particular, he placed more emphasis on the four libertines' social position. In Sade's novel, the libertines are obstinate outsiders who, despite their colossal wealth, exist on the disgraced periphery of eighteenth-century French society, and are largely oblivious to it, except to the degree that it can provide them with human materials for their projects of sexual torture and slaughter. But the libertines of *Salò*, inflected by Pasolini's idiosyncratic version of Marxism, are conceived as 'types', and are clearly fully complicit both with Mussolini's fascist project, and with Italian society in general. The young girls and boys brought to the libertines' villa in *Salò* have all been captured at gunpoint, from peasant farms and wretched urban areas; they are the opposite of Sade's rarefied cast of the abducted children of aristocrats and wealthy military officers.

Despite that difference in emphasis in the social status of the characters in *Salò* and *120 Days of Sodom*, there are close correspondences between the figures of Sade and Pasolini. Even before his imprisonment in the Bastille, Sade had been burned in effigy in the market-place of Aix-en-Provence, after fleeing to Italy to escape being executed for his crimes of sexual debauchery. At the time when *Salò* was made, the openly-homosexual Pasolini had already spent twenty years being reviled by the Italian media for his sexual and political declarations, as well as for the experimentation of his films and books; even in death, he would be assailed and ridiculed by the Italian right-wing media, which unashamedly relished his murder (just as the West German media would relish Fassbinder's cocaine-induced death, seven years later). And both Sade and Pasolini sought, in their disparate ways, to discover means to finally detonate the narratives and foundations of social power-systems.

Pasolini finished the script for *Salò* in February 1975, working with his collaborators Sergio Citti and Pupi Avati. After its casting-sessions, the film was shot very rapidly, over the course of thirty-seven days, from 3 March to 14 April 1975, in a villa near the city of Mantua, not far to the south of the town of Salò. The film was shot with a cast that mixed young, inexperienced actors with veterans of the Italian film-industry, some of them familiar character-actors who would go on to appear in the wave of late-1970s chic Nazi-porn exploitation films which Pasolini's own film unwittingly helped to spark. Before the shooting of each scene, Pasolini only gave instructions at the last moment to the young actors and actresses (most of them non-professionals, who never appeared in any subsequent films) playing the captive boys and girls, thereby inducing an authentic sense of unease and disquiet in their performances. The only break in the gruelling shoot came when Pasolini discovered that Bernardo Bertolucci (whose films, including *Last Tango in Paris*, he detested as crowd-pleasing, consumerist fodder) was shooting his current film, *1900*, in the nearby countryside around Mantua; Bertolucci had briefly served as Pasolini's assistant on a previous film, and *1900* was being produced by the same producer, Alberto Grimaldi, as *Salò*. The football-obsessed Pasolini immediately challenged Bertolucci to a game between the two casts; however, in the subsequent match, marked by violence, the *Salò* cast (captained by the fifty-three-year-old Pasolini, and including the young actors playing the well-endowed 'cockmongers') unexpectedly lost 3-6 to the *1900* team, and Pasolini left the pitch several minutes before the end of the game, exhausted and cursing. Once the filming had been completed, Pasolini moved to other commitments in his writing of fiction, poetry and journalism, returning to the project in early October 1975 to edit it (as with the cinematography of the film, its raw editing shows signs of having been accomplished urgently, while Pasolini's obsessions were still lividly alive), and then travelled to Sweden for screenings of his previous films, and to Paris to prepare a French-language version of *Salò*, before arriving back in Rome on 31 October, the day before his death.

Pasolini was aware that, in many ways, the obscenity and uncompromising cruelty of *Salò* formed a complete break from his earlier films. Although some of those films, especially his first film, *Accatone* (1961), had created scandals of their own, Pasolini knew that *Salò* constituted a new kind of film-making for him. As a result, in 1975, he publicly 'denounced' his previous three films, in order to clear the ground for the reception of *Salò*. Pasolini's previous films had often presented positive and dignified depictions of the poor; in *Salò*, by contrast, the poor and defenceless subjects of torture and slaughter would be relentlessly degraded and excoriated, their status as passive 'victims' provocatively set under interrogative questioning, in order to dismantle it.

Pasolini expected the first screenings of the film to create a furore throughout Europe, and to bring down unprecedented media attacks upon him. He noted: '*Salò* goes so far beyond the limits that those who ordinarily speak badly of me will have to find a new language.'[5] But by the time the film was screened, Pasolini was dead. *Salò* had initially been refused a visa by the Italian censorship board, then passed on 23 December 1975; it was projected in Italian cinemas during the period when newspaper photographs of Pasolini's murdered body – the corpse lying on its front, the mud-caked vest pushed up to reveal its naked back, its chest and head exploded into a pool of blood – were still being avidly consumed by the country's population. After being shown for only three weeks, *Salò* was abruptly withdrawn; for the next three decades, the film faced suppression and censorship-battles in numerous countries around the world, without the presence of Pasolini to defend its driving obsessions.

3.
CIRCLE OF SHIT

The core of *Salò* is the anus, and its narrative drive pivots around the act of sodomy; no scene of a sex act has been confirmed, in the film, until one of the libertines has approached its participants and sodomized the figure committing that act. The filmic material of *Salò* is one that compacts celluloid and shit, in Pasolini's desire to burst the limits of cinema, via the anally resonant eye of the film-lens. In order to achieve an inciting relentlessness in his narrative, and to engulf his victims in the aura of excrement emanated by the film, Pasolini intersects his images with puncture-points of story-tellers' narration. Those story-tellers' sequences in *Salò* carry a more tangential role than that in *120 Days of Sodom*, where they possess a status equal with that of the libertines' acts, in Sade's double-barrelled narrative-technique. In *Salò*, the story-tellers' narratives solely carry the momentum which propels the film's passive victims and viewers into its infernal 'circle of shit'.

In *120 Days of Sodom*, Sade's libertines are all eager shit-eaters, constantly provoking the captive boys and girls to deposit ever-larger consignments of excrement into their mouths, thereby also escalating the number of sex acts which the libertines can accomplish. But the inspiration of Sade's obsession with the human anus extended much further than that of shit-eating, in his influence upon the French Surrealist movement in the 1930s, and on film-makers and theorists of the postwar era, from Pasolini to Gilles Deleuze and Jean Baudrillard. The seminal element in Sade which proved so inspirational is his profound preoccupation with violent anatomical manipulation, with its focus on the anus; once the human body has been radically re-configured, it is in a state of volatile flux which renders it more resistant or unrecuperable to stratified power-formations. In Sade, that reconfiguration of the body is simultaneously both an act of corporeally-endowed power, and the annulment or overturning of that entire structure of power; for example, a libertine, in Sade's book, severs the flesh-partition between a girl's anus and vagina, so that she is forced to defecate through her vagina.

63

Pasolini faltered in his desire to make the young actors and actresses of the *Salò* cast commit un-simulated sodomy and to eat actual excrement, serving them instead a palatable mix of chocolate and orange marmalade, which he retrospectively justified as a material which helped to adhere his film's ability to make connections between elements of consumerism and fascism (in which consumption, even of excrement, is never authentic, and is always the result of a fascistic simulation of the kind denounced by Baudrillard and the Situationist theorists). Until the expansion of the hard-core pornographic industry into shit-eating films at the end of the 1970s, it had been left to experimental film-makers – notably Kurt Kren and Otto Muehl, of the Vienna Action Group, with their seminal work *Scheisskerl* (1970) – to demonstrate that excrement could be eaten, and that act combined with an explicit sex-act, on film.

4.
CIRCLE OF BLOOD

Salò exerts a unique impact of violence and disruption on the viewer's eye, exploring a ground of extreme sensorial disruption more usually associated with non-narrative experimental cinema. The film adroitly manoeuvres the viewer's perspective between that of the victim and that of the torturer, finally situating the viewer firmly in the torture-seat. In *Salò*, the viewer is positioned firmly on the side of monstrosity, and then has a long way back to travel, corporeally and mentally, at the end of the film, if the decision is taken to repudiate that position.

In the final part of *120 Days of Sodom*, Sade's story-tellers range over a vast ground of dismemberment, disembowelment, torture and human eradication, while the libertines, incited by those narratives, perform concurrent acts of torture and killing. Sade's story-tellers recount an entire catalogue of bestiality, some instances of which appear to have been a source of prefiguring inspiration for the performance-acts of the Vienna Action Group: 'This libertine fucks a turkey whose head is gripped between the thighs of a nude, prostrate girl, so it appears he is buggering her. As he pumps away his valet sodomizes him without

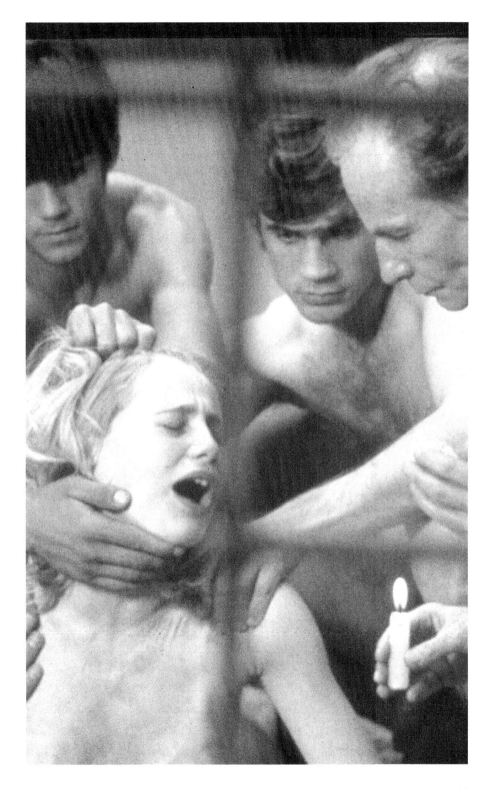

mercy, and at the moment he ejaculates, the girl slits the turkey's throat.'[6] Many of Sade's narrated acts form spectacular performances which evidently have their source in medieval strategies of torture and execution, but also work to compact rituals of killing with obsessional sodomy.

At the end of *120 Days of Sodom*, a careful accounting is made by Sade of the previous four months, detailing the eradication of the children and the numbers of story-tellers and 'cockmongers' who have survived the event. That final calculation is in contrast to the description of the children's intricate slaughter which, even in the fragmentary, unfinished state of Sade's manuscript, always contains minute, lavish detail: 'Next Giton is dragged forth; a burning bodkin is driven through the end of his cock, his remaining testicle is impaled with needles, and four of his teeth gouged out with chisels. Then comes Zelmire, whose death is not far off; a hot poker is run deep into her cunt, six gaping gashes are carved into her tits, and each master pummels her face twenty times with a gloved fist. They rip out four teeth and explode one eye with a skewer, whipping and buggering her for good measure.'[7] The viewer of *Salò*, positioned explicitly by Pasolini into the viewpoint of the binocular-wielding succession of libertines, experiences more fragmentary sequences; the killings of the boys and girls, in the courtyard of the villa, oscillate from close-ups to long-shots, in a volatile rhythm. The acts of slaughter are clearly drawn in large part from those which Pasolini himself had heard of or witnessed in the final stages of the Italian fascist forces' hold on power in 1944-45, and which were common punishments for civilians' acts of support for the partisans: eye-gougings, torture with fire, and anal-rapes followed by execution by hanging. Pasolini's last act in *Salò* is to cut from the slaughter to a tender encounter between two of the young fascists guarding the villa: the two male youths (one of whom is played by Claudio Tròccoli, Pasolini's final lover) dance obliviously, as music from the radio plays.

Pasolini's own violent last act took place seven months after he had filmed that final shot of *Salò*. Many of his friends rejected the official conclusion that he had been battered to death by a lone hustler, and believed instead that he was murdered, in the night of 1-2 November

1975, by agents of the corrupt Italian Christian Democratic Party government, in collusion with neofascist elements; at that time, very little investigation was conducted by the Italian police into Pasolini's killing, and much of the forensic evidence from the site of his death had soon mysteriously disappeared. Thirty years later, it was confirmed by the successors of that government that, from the end of the 1960s until the beginning of the 1980s, at a time of considerable social tension in Italy, it had been covertly organizing and inciting acts of terrorism and of murder, with the aim of terrifying and subjugating the Italian population into supporting that government's repressive, right-wing agenda, against which Pasolini had fiercely protested. As yet, however, no confirmation has ever been made that Pasolini's killing was executed or directly 'facilitated' by the Italian government or its neofascist associates.

Three weeks after Pasolini had completed the editing of *Salò*, and on the day after he had returned to Rome from Paris, where he had worked on the film's French-language version, he picked up a seventeen-year-old hustler, Giuseppe Pelosi, late on the evening of 1 November 1975, outside Rome's Stazione Termini central railway-station. On the afternoon of that same day, Pasolini had given his final interview, noting: 'In a certain sense, we are all weak because we are all victims. And are guilty because all are ready for the massacre game...'.[8] Pasolini offered Pelosi the modest sum of twenty thousand lire, and then drove him in his Alfa Romeo Giulia 2000 sports-car to isolated waste-ground near the sea at Ostia, to the west of Rome, where Pasolini sucked the boy's penis, with the two men still seated in the car. After Pasolini and Pelosi had exited the car to continue their sex act in the wasteland, Pasolini was abruptly attacked, and had his penis and testicles kicked with such violence that he suffered a severe internal haemorrhage; he then had his head clubbed so savagely with a wooden plank that his skull burst open, and brain-matter stuck to the plank. As he lay on the ground, he had his upper body driven-over by his own car, and died instantly from (as the autopsy stated) 'tearing-apart of the chest' (his heart literally burst under the pressure of the car's weight) and the crushing of his skull. The hustler Pelosi then drove off in the stolen car, stopped at a water-fountain in

Ostia to wash Pasolini's blood from his clothes, and then sped off on the highway towards Rome in an exhilarated frenzy; he was almost immediately arrested and detained by the police for speeding, and confessed to the killing later that day. Pasolini had remained where he fell until he was discovered on the wasteland at dawn, on his front, one arm trapped under his body, his chest and skull almost flattened-down to the level of the ground, a foot-wide pool of congealed blood like a mythic halo around his head.

At Pelosi's trial, it was finally decided that he had acted alone. But the severity of the attack on Pasolini indicated the likelihood that Pelosi had been working in collaboration with four of his hustler-associates from the Stazione Termini, with whom he had talked briefly, at the railway-station's bar, before then leaving for the Ostia wasteland with Pasolini. The group of five hustlers may have attacked Pasolini simply in order to rob him, or the killing may have been a kind of initiation ceremony for Pelosi (many of the Stazione Termini hustlers were murderous thugs, and carried greater prestige after having accomplished their first act of killing), in which Pasolini had the misfortune to be the 'old faggot' who was in the wrong place at the wrong time; in that scenario, the other four hustlers drove separately to Ostia, trailing the Alfa Romeo Giulia 2000 sports-car carrying Pasolini and Pelosi, and then all five hustlers attacked Pasolini together, holding him down to beat his head with the plank. Although Pasolini was over fifty, he remained tough and muscled from his regular football games, so it was unlikely that one young hustler alone could have inflicted so much damage to his body. Pelosi served seven years of a nine-year prison-sentence for the murder; after his release in 1983, he undertook a career as a criminal, committing robberies and acts of violence, and gave magazine and television interviews about his role in Pasolini's killing; he never admitted the participation of other hustlers in the murder, and, in his later years, even denied his own involvement. He died aged 59 in 2017 in Rome of lung cancer.

A final scenario, raised by Pasolini's more pessimistic friends at the time of his death, was the possibility of an intentional suicide, orchestrated by Pasolini himself, in his despair at the dissipation, by

1975, of the 1960s' riotous momentum towards revolutionary social change, and the onset of a terminally consumerist, media-dominated Italian society, which increasingly mocked and dismissed Pasolini's work.

Whether Pasolini was murdered by the Italian government's agents and neofascist associates, by one hustler alone, or by five hustlers together, or as a result of his own suicidal desire, the story of his killing, in the end, is reduced to the status of Sade's bare, notational narrative-fragments in Parts Two to Four of *120 Days of Sodom*. The account given of that killing by Pelosi's trial-judge (a lenient judge, like Sade himself), drawing from Pelosi's testimony, resonates with the relentless narrational momentum of Sade's story-tellers at the Castle of Silling: 'Pelosi added that Pasolini brought him to the playing field; that Pasolini took Pelosi's penis in his mouth for a moment but did not finish the blow-job; that he made Pelosi get out of the car and came up behind him, squeezing him from behind and trying to lower his trousers; that Pelosi told him to stop and instead Pasolini picked up a stake of the kind used for garden-fences and tried to put it up his behind, or at least he stuck it against his behind though without even lowering his trousers; that Pelosi turned around and told him he was crazy; that Pasolini by now was without his glasses, which he had left in the car, and on looking him in the face it seemed to Pelosi so much the face of a madman that he was frightened; that he tried to run but stumbled and fell; that he felt Pasolini on top of him, hitting him on the head with a stick; that he grabbed the stick and flung Pasolini away from him; that he again started running, and again was caught and struck on the temple and various parts of the body; that he noticed a plank on the ground, picked it up and broke it over Pasolini's head; that he also kicked him once or twice "in the balls"; that Pasolini seemed not even to feel those kicks; that then Pasolini grabbed him and struck him again on the nose; that Pelosi no longer saw what he was doing and repeatedly hit Pasolini with the plank until he heard him wheezing to the ground; that he ran in the direction of the car carrying the two broken pieces of plank and the stake, which he threw away near the car; that he got immediately into the car and fled in it; that he did not know whether or not in his escape he had run over Pasolini's body with the car... and that during these events, he and Pasolini had always been alone.'[9]

In his death, and in his final act as a film-maker with *Salò*, Pier Paulo Pasolini confirmed a definitive declaration he had made in an interview several years earlier: 'I love life fiercely, desperately. And I believe that this fierceness, this desperation will carry me to the end... How will it all end? I don't know.'[10]

1. Stack, Oswald, *Pasolini on Pasolini*, Thames and Hudson, (London), 1969, pp.55-56.
2. Siciliano, Enzo, *Pasolini*, Bloomsbury (London), 1987, p.386.
3. Marquis de Sade, *120 Days of Sodom*, Solar Books (London), 2008, p.21.
4. Pasolini, interview with Gideon Bachmann from April 1975, 'Pasolini on De Sade', *Film Quarterly* (Berkeley), issue of Winter 1975-76, p.41.
5. ibid, p.41.
6. *120 Days of Sodom*, p.248.
7. ibid, p.284.
8. Pasolini, interview with Furio Colombo, from the afternoon of 1 November 1975, for the newspaper arts supplement 'Tutto libro' (Turin), quoted in Schwartz, Barth David, *Pasolini Requiem*, Pantheon, New York, 1992, p.649.
9. *Pasolini*, pp.8-9.
10. ibid (interview with the French magazine *Lui*, April 1970), p.359.

MEDICO-LEGAL REPORT ON PIER PAOLO PASOLINI'S BODY

A forensic report by Professor Faustino Durante, 1975

ON PASOLINI'S BODY BEING RUN OVER BY HIS OWN CAR

As first thing, I would like to point out that a precise reconstruction of the acts that led to Pasolini's death must take into account the following elements: 1) the photographs taken on the death scene before the body was taken away to study the position of the body as a whole, of the single parts of the body (head, upper limbs, torso, lower limbs) in relation to the murder scene, and to study the position of the clothes still worn by the victim, and of the visible body injuries, together with all the traces of tyres leading up to the body; 2) the injuries on and under the skin, the bone, endothoracic (heart) and endoabdominal organs (liver) injuries; 3) the metal parts of the car. As stated by their own admission in the experts' report, the professors who wrote it down, stated they found it extremely difficult to carry out a detailed reconstruction of the scene adding that their "decision" about the dynamics of the incident that led to Pasolini's death takes origin only from the observation of certain anatomopathological aspects: the very few and irregular rib fractures, the rupture of the heart with no pericardial rupture, the absence of skin bruises matching with the tyre patterns. Yet there are no references in the experts' report to the rupture of the liver, the characteristics of the single skin injuries, and, above all, to each group of injuries, examined singularly and in connection with all the other injuries. Besides, there is no comparison between the photographs of Pasolini's body before it was removed from the murder scene and the areas surrounding the corpse.

A careful investigation systematically carried out by analysing all the available elements – according to the above-mentioned method – takes into account the following considerations.

FROM THE NECROSCOPIC EXAMINATION:

a) Presence of "ferrous material" on the vest, on the head, neck, shoulders and on the upper limbs "especially on the lateral surfaces" (pages 4 and 5 of the report). This material is not present on the lower part of the vest and on the trousers.

b) Presence of two large and similar ecchymotic bruises on the lateral frontal regions (pages 6, 11, 12, 14 of the report).

c) Excoriated ecchymosis on the left zygomatic and masseter region (page 5 of the report).

d) Fracture in two parts of the left horizontal section of the jaw and dislocation of the left temporomandibular joint (pages 15 and 16 of the report). Absence of injuries on the right section of the jaw.

e) The nasal pyramid appears flattened from the left to the right (page 11 of the report).

f) Transversal injury on the right ear (pages 16, 18 of the report). There are no skin alterations in the areas above the ear.

g) Presence on the right occipitoparietal region of a "series of 2 cm – 4,5 cm long double linear, roughly transversal and parallel injuries, the first – characterised by three continuous marks – located on the back of the ear, the second – characterised by four continuous marks – located in a more central part, roughly near the head midline...", the injuries "flare towards the lower part", and the flaring is "more marked in the injuries in the middle" (pages 18, 19 of the report).

h) Large injury on the front and back of the left ear. This injury flares "especially in the lower part" (pages 23, 24 of the report).

i) Injury on the left ear. The ear is "almost entirely torn out" and covered in an injury around "the upper middle third" (page 25).

l) Swelling of the left lateral cervical region with "mainly transversal" bruises in a row (pages 25, 26 of the report).

m) Various bruises on the back areas of the left shoulder, on the back in a "transversal" or "oblique" position (page 28 of the report); not seeped in blood and not "reproducing" the shape or pattern of the object that provoked them (pages 28 and 29 of the report). "These bruises extend towards the lumbar region since the hemorrhagic infiltration is more marked in the injuries located in this part of the body and at the base of the left emithorax" (page 29 of the report).

n) Transversal bruises at the base of the emithoraxes, on the front and on the abdomen (pages 31, 32, 33 of the report). Not steeped in blood.

o) Bruises in correspondence of the left anterior superior iliac spine. This area developed an ecchymosis (page 33 of the report).

p) Various bruises around the anterior emithoraxes, not seeped in blood (pages 31, 32, 33, 34 of the report).

q) Continuous injury on the left arm (pages 36 and 37 of the report).

r) "Group of injuries in the shape of a rough 6 cm x 3 cm lozenge that, on an ecchymotic background, presents red-greyish abrasions" (page 37 of the report, on the back of the left forearm).

s) Ecchymotic group of bruises on the back of the left hand with fractures of some phalanx bones and a cut on the index finger (page 40 of the report).

t) Fracture of the breast bone at the level of the III space; fracture of the IV and V right rib along the emiclavear line, fracture of the VII and VIII right rib along the back armpit line; on the left side, fracture of the VI and VII ribs in two different parts; along the emiclavear line and on the front armpit line, fracture of the VIII and IX rib on the front armpit line. As a whole there were 10 rib fractures (page 48 of the report).

u) 15cm and 7cm long capsular hepatic lacerations on the frontal-lateral surface of the right lobe and on the surface of the left lobe (page 51 of the report).

v) Absence of hematic infiltrations inside the walls of the thorax, of the abdomen and of every region of the lower limbs (page 51 and following pages of the report).

FROM THE PHOTOGRAPHIC EXAMINATION:

Pasolini's body is lying face down; the head is resting on the ground

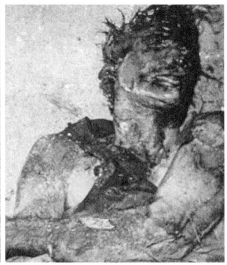

touching it with the lateral left regions and, more precisely, with the temporal, frontal and zygomatic regions and with the chin. The nasal pyramid is flattened towards the right side. The right frontal and zygomatic region and the chin are exposed. The left arm is slightly distanced from the rest of the body and bent at the elbow, so that the following parts can be seen: a lateral portion of the arm and its back, the elbow and a lateral portion and the back of the upper middle third of the forearm. The right arm is positioned under the body so only the palm of the hand coming out from the left side of the body can be seen. The victim is wearing a vest that leaves the back partially uncovered; the vest is slightly ripped only in one place on the right side; the trousers are not ripped; the shoes are untouched.

The head and right hand injuries can not be clearly seen. Various oblique rows of bruises crossing the body from the lower to the upper part and from the right to the left along the left hip can clearly be seen, together with other bruises, that are not so oblique in this case, appearing on the lumbar region of the spine.

Traces of tyres that lead to Pasolini's body can be seen clearly enough; one tyre trace marks the lumbar region of the spine, around the upper middle third of the body. This left mark appears diagonally on the body, from the lower to the upper part and from the right to the left.

BY EXAMINING PASOLINI'S CAR:

Examining the internal part of the car it results that the lower point – the first muffler of the exhaust pipe – is located at 12 cm from the ground; the second muffler is located at 13cm from the ground. Besides, two parts with very narrow sides, namely the section jutting out of the metal strut of the left side of the car and the support of the stabilising bar on the same side, are located at 14 cm and 13,5 cm from the ground.

FROM THE OBJECTIVE DATA GATHERED ABOVE WE CAN DRAW THE FOLLOWING CONSIDERATIONS:

The sides and the back of Pasolini's body and, more precisely, the head, neck, shoulders, the back and the lumbar region, are covered in groups of injuries – bruises more or less seeping in blood and wounds characterised by skin lacerations or contusions and lacerations – that, singularly or in group, cross the body at times transversally and at others obliquely, from the right to the left side or from the bottom to the top.

The various groups of injuries form three rows of almost parallel lines distributed in this way on the body: slightly oblique lines around the head from the bottom to the top and from the right to the left (from the injury on the right ear that covers the lower third to the injury on the left ear covering the upper middle third), numerous almost transversal cuts around the right occipital region and the rather large avulsion injury around the left occipital-parietal region up to the left ear avulsion. [Letters f); g); h); i)]; injuries around the neck, the left shoulder and the upper part of the back with a partially transversal, partially oblique pattern again from the bottom to the top and from the right to the left side [letters l); m)]; injuries around the lower part and around the lower back region and the lumbar region with a pattern similar to the one described above [letter m)].

The way the injuries appear on the body leads us to believe that blunt objects were probably employed to produce the transversal injuries, and this hypothesis becomes more likely if compared to the peculiar characteristics of each injury and to the characteristics of other injuries on the skin, bones or on the internal organs.

Starting from the head and carrying on from the right to the left, we should pay attention to the following elements:

The right ear injury is transversal, it looks like an injury provoked by a cutting device or like an avulsion lesion, and does not present skin abrasions on the upper part. This leads us to think that the injury was produced transversally, excluding an action from the bottom to the top that would have "ripped" the lobe from the lower part of the ear continuing towards the auricle;

This ripped laceration appears instead laterally towards the left side, that is on the nearby nape region, where there are numerous injuries all in the same direction, that is transversally or with a slightly oblique pattern from the bottom to the top; all the injuries flare around the lower part, especially those injuries located around the central part of the nape area. This is caused by two reasons: first of all, this area is located at a higher distance from the ground and therefore the device used to hurt the body acted in depth while proceding forward; then, in this point the nape area curves, so the blunt object ended up hurting a rather convex surface.

Further on towards the left, towards the left occipital-parietal region, a large avulsion flares around the lower and lateral part, detaching the ear. The ear is also transversally sectioned off. The characteristics of the injuries to the head that were so far listed lead us to believe that, when the car ran over Pasolini's body, the latter was lying on the ground with the right side of the head touching it, so that the first metallic structures that hit the body collided with the left parieto-occipital-auricular section producing vast lacerations to the scalp and the detachment of the ear; the collision also rotated the head, so that further metal parts touched the central and right parts of the nape; as the head rotated, the metal parts collided with the right part of the face, transversally lacerating the right ear.

To complete the reconstruction, let's make a comparison with the characteristics of other injuries, first and foremost remembering the injuries that follow: the bruised ecchymosis with similar characteristics located on the lateral frontal regions; the fracture of the left section of the jaw and the temporal-jaw dislocation on the same side; the fracture of the nasal bones and the deviation by crushing of the nasal pyramid towards the right side; the position of the head of the victim that appeared touching the ground with the left side.

The complete dynamics of the accident derives therefore from this attempted reconstruction. The first collision with the metal parts produced indeed, indirectly, the bruised-grazed abrasion with laceration on the right frontal region resting on the ground; after rotating, the head ended up for quite a short time resting on the ground with the nose and the chin; on that exact moment another metallic device arrived colliding with the nape (where it also produced some injuries, the ones around the centre of the nape) and compressed the head fracturing the nasal bones; afterwards, while the head kept on rotating but the compression continued, the left section of the jaw – the only resistance point between the ground and the compressive strength coming from the back – broke. The right section did not get fractured because the head in this short time, as already stated, was rotating and therefore the point of resistance between the two forces, that is the ground and the compressive strength from the back, was the left section of the jaw.

The right ear was injured immediately afterwards, causing, on the other side, an injury on the left frontal part where a bruised ecchymosis also appeared with a skin lesion; at the same time the nose was squashed towards the right side. The medium frontal region was not affected by large injuries because it never touched the ground; even when the face was lying on the ground, the points that protruded the most were the nose and the chin.

For what regards the injuries on the lateral-back region of the neck, their transversal and oblique direction – together with the fact that they appear "in rows" – was unmistakably produced by a device that, creeping, moved transversally on the body.

The same considerations can be made for the numerous abrasions on the back of the left shoulder, the back region and the lumbar region. All of them have a transversal and oblique direction according to the experts who describe the lower ones as presenting a "more marked hemorrhagic infiltration". This detail clearly indicates the action of an object that bruised and compressed, like a tyre.

Other considerable injuries on the upper left limb and on the arm must also be taken into account to understand from which direction the body was run over. Bearing in mind that, when the body was found, the upper limb was bent at the elbow's level, it is likely that the above-mentioned injuries were produced by the metal parts, even though it shouldn't be excluded the compressive action of the tyres at least for what concerns some of the bruises.

At the end of this attempted reconstruction it must be remembered that among the various injuries on the back of the head, the large laceration flaring towards the lower part on the left side of the nape, for its characteristics may have been produced by a blunt object that caused a trauma directly before the body of the victim was run over by the car. Anyway we will go back to this detail later on.

Considering the specific problem of the tyres passing onto the body of the victim, it must be remembered that, apart from the above-mentioned injuries on the back, there were various injuries on the front of the body, mostly seeped in blood, and one abrasion with ecchymosis by the left antero-superior iliac spine. The autoptic examination did not reveal any hemorrhagic infiltrations in the thoracic and abdominal walls, but showed that there were 10 rib fractures, the rupture of the heart and two liver lacerations, one rather large (15 cm).

In all the injuries (skin, bone and internal organ injuries on the front and back), there are the typical marks caused by tyres running over a body, as they appear in road accidents; there are very few external injuries mainly represented by abrasions not seeped in blood and a few ecchymoses in the areas with bones underneath (like the areas around the left iliac spine and the last left ribs), the internal injuries are rather extended and include bone fractures and internal organ ruptures. It's not possible in this case to state that the fractures in the rib area are "relatively mild" (pages 76, 77 of the experts' report) since there are 10 rib fractures; nor it is possible to agree with the part in which the report talks about the "irregular distribution of the points of fracture" (page 77 of the experts' reports) taking into account the distribution lines (right and left emiclaver, left anterior and right back armpit line), the points of fracture (IV, V, VII and VIII rib on the right side; VI, VII, VIII and IX ribs on the left), and also the sternal fracture that occurred around the level of a rib fracture, third intercostal space.

In the same way, it is not possible to agree with the report stating that the injuries regarding the internal organs are not serious (page 77 of the report) since there were a heart rupture and liver lacerations (the latter were never included by the experts into their considerations).

The medico-legal traumatology and the data collected in previous road accidents do not show that tyres running over a human body absolutely cause "thoracic rupture" and the "laceration of the pericardium" or anyway "much more serious injuries, consequence of the rupture of the internal organs" (page 77 of the report). Medical practice and experience show that the consequences can be – as it happened in this specific case – 10 rib fractures, a sternal fracture, the heart rupture and two liver lacerations.

For what regards the absence of prints of the tyre patterns on the skin or on the garments, previous cases revealed that this is actually rather ordinary.

In a nutshell, from all the gathered elements it appears as more likely that Pasolini's body was run over by his own car in accordance with the following dynamics: the car, arriving from the right side of the body, obliquely ran over it with the left wheels, in a direction that went from the top to the bottom and from the right to the left along an ideal line that, from the lower part of the costal arch reached the left scapular region; the wheels produced skin injuries around the spine and lumbar regions (on the latter there were the typical injuries produced by the external edge of the tyres), indirect skin injuries to the abdomen and the thorax, two liver lacerations, rib fractures, sternal fracture and rupture of the heart. As the tyres ran over the body, the metal parts directly produced various lacerated and bruised injuries to the head, the transversal injury on the ears, the detachment of the left ear; the rows of abrasion on the back of the left side of the neck; and, indirectly, the fractures of the left section of the jaw, the fracture of the nasal bones and cartilages, the bruised ecchymoses and the skin lacerations on the frontal regions; they probably also produced some injuries on the upper left limb.

It is not very likely that the car ran over the body in a caudo-cranial direction without passing over it with the wheels, but only touching it with the metal parts for the following reasons:

1) absence of "ferrous material" (not identified by the experts) coming from the metal parts of the car on the trousers of the victim;

2) no rips on the trousers;

3) absence of ample and numerous rips on the vest caused by the protruding metal parts as you would expect from the above-mentioned reconstruction;

4) absence of any injury on the external tissues and on the bones of the pelvis and of the lower limbs, considering that very strong structures such as the metal strut of the car's lateral frame are located at a distance of 14 cm and 13,5 cm, while the distance between the upper part of the buttocks and the ground in a subject with Pasolini's body frame is roughly 18-20 cm; and the distance from the back of the thighs to the ground is roughly 14 cm. We should also point out that other metal parts of the car are located at 12-13 cm from the ground;

5) absence of injuries caused by the scalp being torn from the bottom to the top; such injuries would have been produced when the metal parts with large surfaces and sharply defined edges – such as the two silencers of the exhaust pipes – collided with the head;

6) absence of vast skin injuries on the back – again from the bottom to the top – considering the distance from the ground of the metal parts and the thickness of Pasolini's thorax – 23 cm (page 45 of the experts' report).

DYNAMICS OF THE ATTACK. HYPOTHESIS ON THE PRESENCE OF MORE THAN JUST ONE ATTACKER.

While agreeing with the experts stating it was rather difficult to identify the objects that produced the injuries on the victim's body, we must point out that such statements should never exclude a detailed examination of every objective element to be able to produce at least some hypotheses.

The objective elements of major interest identified while analysing the exhibits, the data gathered on the murder scene and the examination of all the groups of injuries, are the following ones:

1) the shortest pole (around 40,5 cm long) is completely covered in blood and groups of Pasolini's hair are stuck on its extremities;

2) the longest pole (58 cm) presents a little spot of Pasolini's blood;

3) the wood board on which there is written "Buttinelli A." is still covered in blood and also presents groups of Pasolini's hair in four different places;

4) the "left third" of the bottom edge of the wooden board with the street indication "Via Idroscalo 93" is entirely covered in blood; traces of Pasolini's hair also appear on the back surface;

5) there are Pasolini's hair and blood encrustations also on the trapezoid wooden fragment that came off the above-mentioned board;

6) Pasolini's striped shirt (found at around 70 metres from the body) is largely drenched in blood on the back and on the sleeves, while there are few spots of blood on the front;

7) on the left cuff of Pelosi's wool top the reddish spot (that later was identified as Pasolini's blood), is not "large" (page 15 of the experts' report) but it measures just a few centimeters in length and width;

8) the spot of blood (that later was identified as Pelosi's) found on the front edge of Pelosi's vest, extends for around 3 cm;

9) the lower part of the right leg of Pelosi's trousers is not "largely stained" (page 14 of the experts' report) with blood (that then resulted as Pasolini's), but it presents various blood stains mixed with a large quantity of mud;

10) none of the garments worn by Pelosi – except the left cuff of the shirt and the bottom of the right leg of the above-mentioned trousers – present traces of Pasolini's blood;

11) the injury to Pelosi's head did not present any ecchymotic or bruised areas;

12) before being arrested, Pelosi, on board Pasolini's car, that he was driving at high speed, was "trapped" against a pavement by a police car;

13) Pasolini's body was found at 70 metres from his shirt that appeared

as if it had been normally taken off;

14) near the shirt there were two fragments of the stick and two halves of the wooden board;

15) the board was found near the spot where Pasolini's body was found;

16) there were traces of Pasolini's blood on the roof of his car.

Regarding the injuries on Pasolini's body, please refer to the first part of this report.

Based on the gathered data and from what can be seen from the photographs of the murder scene, it is possible to draw the following considerations.

The blunt objects found on the murder scene, the two pieces of wood and the two boards, were certainly used to hit Pasolini's body. We can claim that at least four or five of the injuries on the back were caused by these objects. The characteristics of some of the injuries such as the limited amount of blood infiltrating them, together with their irregular shapes, and the bruises that developed from them, or the characteristics of other injuries, such as the ecchymoses along the edges, and the direction of the flaring, takes us to consider them as produced using an object with a wide surface (board) or a narrow surface (the edge of a board and a stick).

It is also likely that a direct blow delivered by a blunt object caused the bruised ecchymotic section on the left zygomatic area and the roughly rectangular bruised ecchymotic region under the right gonion, the L-shaped bruised ecchymosis found near the right shoulder and the multiple bruises and ecchymoses on the upper limbs, plus the fractures of the phalanx bones that according to the findings on the murder scene regarding the position of the body, can not be attributed to the body being run over by a car.

Considering the poor resistance offered by the stick (a dry and crumbly material) and relatively also by the board, the hypothesis of the action of other objects acquires credibility.

The fractures on the phalanx bones lead to the hypothesis of another blunt object, more solid than the others found on the murder scene, and to this end we must take into consideration also the wide laceration with missing parts and tissues (in such large quantities that, in the experts' report, this wound is described as having unmatchable margins) and flaring towards the lower part on the left nape area. As stated in the first chapter, this injury for its characteristics leads us to consider it as produced by a tangential movement from the top to the bottom, so we can not exclude that the injury may have been produced in this phase of the attack, but certainly by a weapon much more solid than the stick and the board.

The hypothesis contemplating the use of other blunt objects during the attack becomes more likely when some elements of the murder scene are taken into consideration: the spot where Pasolini's shirt was found (70 metres from the body), the blood spots on the shirt, the fact that the shirt was not ripped, the spot where the board was used and the spot where the stick was used.

A careful examination of these elements takes us to a first unquestionable reconstruction of the dynamics of the attack: at first Pasolini was violently struck by a blow on the head in a spot located at around 70 metres from the spot where his body fell, and the injuries copiously bled. The unquestionable proof is the fact that the shirt was drenched in blood and was found in a spot located at around 70 metres from the body. The shirt was not ripped and this indicates that the victim had removed it by himself after he covered himself with his arms (the sleeves were drenched in blood) or after he tried to defend himself.

What kind of object was used to cause so many vast injuries?

It is actually rather difficult to answer this question if we consider the stick as the only weapon used in this attack, highlighting that in the first stage of the attack the board on the Buttinelli wooden gate located at roughly 70 metres (where Pasolini's body was found) was not used, and that it was therefore used in the second stage of the attack.

It is therefore possible that there was a second blunt object used in the first stage of the attack.

But it is also possible that there was more than just one attacker.

We must indeed wonder at this stage who used the other blunt object and, above all, we must still explain the absence of blood traces on the front of Pelosi's clothes (if we do not take into consideration a spot of blood on the left cuff of his top) since this first stage of the attack would have produced a copious hemorrhage.

The scalp is well vascularised and that kind of hemorrhage or the injuries that produced it usually touch arterial vases provoking acute oozing bleeding.

These doubts increase when we pass to examine the second stage of the attack in which the board was employed. The board repetitively hit the victim flat and at an angle and the victim was also struck on his head (Pasolini's hair was stuck to different areas of the board); the board is 75 cm long, but on one of the larger surfaces there was a large spot of blood with quite a few hairs, that leads us to think it was used to violently strike the victim, producing a large oozing bleeding that strangely didn't smear Pelosi's garments. On the other hand, it seems rather unlikely that the attack with blunt objects was repetitively carried out on larger limbs!

In a nutshell, while it may not be possible to exclude Pelosi's active presence from the murder scene, as this is proved by the spot of blood on the cuff of his shirt and by some stains on the lower edge of his trousers, we can almost certainly state that he was not alone since his clothes were only moderately stained, which puzzles even those with very little experience in such reconstructions.

We do not think it necessary – even though we reserve ourselves the right to do it in other circumstances – to produce texts or criminology works and photographic evidence of the scientific police that can be used as relevant examples for this case, but we would like to stress the type of blood splattering usually produced in places where a victim is violently struck upon the head with blunt objects. In conclusion, there are two relevant objective elements that lead us to believe there were almost certainly other attackers on the murder scene and that further objects were employed: the disproportion between the wooden stick that produced the wounds on the scalp and the entity of the same injuries; the wide hemorrhage that took place during the first stage of the attack and the limited amount of blood stains on Pelosi's clothes.

We must also take care of another element that is also part of all the various hypotheses about the dynamics of the murder, and that's the fact that Pasolini reacted very little or did not react at all, and the consequent attack was determined by that inaction. Pasolini definitely received a violent blow to the testicles. Now, if he received this blow in the first stage of the attack, it prevented Pasolini from reacting, leaving him at the mercy of his attacker, not allowing him, since he was repetitively struck on the head, to remove his shirt, stand up and walk for around 70 metres; the attacker on the other hand would have been able to keep on beating him with the same stick until leaving the victim dying. If, on the contrary, as it may seem more likely, the blow on the testicles was delivered in the second stage of the attack when Pasolini fell unconscious on the ground, and then the attacker continued hitting him with the board, then it really becomes unlikely that in the first stage there was no fight between the victim and the attacker; during the fight the bodies must have been close one to the other, and this would contradict the fact that there were relatively few stains of blood on Pelosi's clothes.

From the laboratory analyses it was found out that the blood traces inside Pasolini's car, in the same case as the traces on Pelosi's vest, belonged to Pelosi. We can therefore draw two hypotheses: either Pelosi took part in a fight with Pasolini, but in this case he couldn't have been alone because his clothes were too "clean" as stated earlier on; or the injury on Pelosi's frontal region was produced later on, more likely when Pelosi banged his head against the wheel, as it was stated earlier on, after he was "trapped" against a pavement by a police car while driving Pasolini's car at high speed. However, this second hypothesis implies an absolute lack of any reaction from Pasolini and therefore the presence of other people becomes in this case very likely.

There are still some doubts about Pasolini's blood, described by the experts as "little and small blood stains" on the roof of his car and, more precisely, near the edge of the roof around the back of the right door.

It is clear that also for this objective data we can put forward two hypotheses: either the blood was "left" in that spot directly by Pasolini himself or it was "taken" there indirectly by the attacker. In the first case – considering the distance from the ground of the place where the blood traces were found and the presence of a metal part with a sharp edge such as the water drip – we may guess that Pasolini's head banged against it during the attack, but this hypothesis seems to be contradicted by the absence of other biological (hair) elements, even though we should take into consideration the time that passed between the facts and the experts' analysis of the car.

It is possible that – still in the context of the first hypothesis – during the attack, Pasolini was thrown against the car, the upper parts of his torso collided with his car splashing blood on its roof, or that, during the attack, Pasolini found himself standing near his car and leant on it with a hand already covered in blood.

In both the cases, though, there is a new dynamics of the attack that does not find any correspondence in Pelosi's statement. The latter described indeed a very first stage marked by Pasolini's aggressiveness near the fencing net (around 20 metres from the spot where the car was parked) that developed along several metres (around 50 metres in the direction of the spot where Pasolini's body was found), and during this stage Pelosi started reacting.

Now, if we consider as absolutely unreliable Pelosi's version since there weren't on his body and on his clothes any traces of violent blows, we have once again a sort of "gap" in the first stage of the attack, that is we are left once again with a question mark about the developments of the very first part of the attack while the hypothesis of a first "very eventful" stage near the car (presence of shirt drenched in blood, repeated use of the stick or anyway of a blunt object, Pasolini's blood on the roof of his car) becomes more likely, together with the hypothesis of an attack carried out by more than one person, since it is very unlikely – for the above mentioned reasons – that Pelosi violently reacted at first alone against the defenceless Pasolini.

If Pelosi "took" Pasolini's blood on the roof of his car, we would have to wonder why only Pelosi's hands were covered in blood, and why did he have to move towards the right side of the car.

In conclusion, the in-depth examination of all the objective data (location, Pelosi's interrogations, exhibits, stick, board, clothes, Pasolini's injuries) shows on one side that Pelosi's statements on the dynamic of the entire attack are unreliable and leads us to consider as likely the hypothesis that Pasolini was the victim of an attack carried out by more than one person.

Pelosi and police at Pasolini's death site.

PORNO-TEO-KOLOSSAL

An essay by Alessandra Fagioli

1.
THE LAST HELL: *PORNO-TEO-KOLOSSAL*

Shortly after the editing of *Salò* and a few months before dying, Pasolini wrote with Sergio Citti a script for a "film on ideology" that was meant to represent three different kinds of utopia, linked to a pre-industrial past, a neocapitalist present and a technocratic future, inexorably destined to fail through apocalyptic catastrophes that would have brought people to the end of the last utopia, the utopia of Faith.

The narration of *Porno-Teo-Kolossal* (1975), as metaphorical and ideological as that of *Salò* and as complex and endless as that of *Petrolio* (Oil), develops through a fantastic and hallucinated trip (that partly calls back to mind Totò and Ninetto's "surreal" journey in *Uccellacci e Uccellini* ("The Hawks and The Sparrows"), and partly recalls the "evangelical" journey of Saint Paul in the eponymous yet never released project), made by Nunzio and Epifanio (Ninetto Davoli and Eduardo De Filippo) who are following a Comet (the Ideology) journeying to the place where the Messiah was born. The purpose of this slave-master (rather than father-son) pilgrimage is therefore religious (the advent of the Saviour) and is not prompted by a political disappointment (the end of Marxism), so that the "journey" through three metaphorical cities with a final destination in the Orient, brings the characters to the acknowledgement of a "reality" that coincides with the end of every utopia.

It is even more important that, to tell a story with a strong ideological-symbolic meaning, in which different genres (magic fable, picaresque tale, erotic story and Biblical apologue) are mixed together,

Pasolini adopts almost exclusively the language of the body, developing different aspects referring to sexuality: from the prohibition-transgression-punishment cycle to the relation between permissiveness and repression; from the discovery of homophile or heterophile eroticism to the exemplary correction or the capital execution; from the scandal for not respecting a prohibition to the most violent phallocratic form of violence.

Nunzio and Epifanio's journey towards the land of the Messiah unrolls following a perfectly symmetrical and mirroring structure, through which the director builds three realities, each inspired by a different type of utopia, according to the fictional setting that characterises them. The antagonism between Sodom/Rome and Gomorrah/Milan is first of all considered on a historical-political level, juxtaposing Rome in the '50s, still untouched by the monsters of the industrialisation and with a lifestyle based on "real" principles of tolerance and democracy, to Milan in the mid-'70s, a city characterised by a total loss of values caused by neocapitalism and governed by the most bitter forms of violence and terror. In both the cities power is exercised through two juxtaposed forms of sexual coercion each implying a corresponding hetero-erotic excitement, from which derives a vision of sex as a discriminating element between granted freedom, imposed habit and punitive regime. If, indeed, homosexual male and female couples represent the norm in Sodom, heterosexual couples are confined in the Quartiere Borghese (Middle Class District), where they are anyway tolerated by a rather friendly and benevolent police force (more prone to issuing advice rather than prohibitions), Gomorrah is ruled by a phallocratic regime that not only allows but actually imposes violent sexual relationships between men and women, including aggressive and vandalous acts, savagely punishing any form of clandestine homophilia.

In this antithetical setting also national holidays (obviously based on sexual abuses), somehow reflect the nature of the ruling governments: Sodom celebrates the Feast of Fertilisation consisting in a yearly and exhilaratingly collective sexual act during which men and women copulate to guarantee the continuity of the species, tolerating racial and heterosexual minorities; Gomorrah celebrates instead the Feast of the Initiation during which hordes of naked youth possessed by a brutal hate and a blind wickedness are set free after a long captivity and encouraged to seize the city through any kind of violence (for example raping, robbing and looting).

Having created these two utopias – one relating to meekness and tolerance, represented by Sodom, and one relating to violence and cruelty incarnated by Gomorrah – Pasolini inserts in both of them an "anomaly of the destiny" that manifests itself through the transgression of the norm provoked by the discovery of true passion, that is the experience of homosexual or heterosexual coitus, depending on the coercion suffered. Both these "anomalies" take place when Epifanio sleeps in an inn and therefore does not see what is happening, transforming in this way the subjective point of view (through which the national holidays and the exemplary punishments are represented) into an objective one that actually ends up revealing the most intense and meaningful moments in the story.

In Sodom, during a ball in which male and female participants are dancing rigorously separated, a boy and a girl realise they are "mysteriously" attracted by each other, and abandon themselves to the pleasures of the heterosexual coitus: "... this is very poetical because they discover love and therefore sex in its original purity. Yet this is also an erotically charged moment because they discover the most carnal instincts and the profound excitement that they can unleash." The city is essentially governed by meek and benevolent rules, so once the two lovers are discovered, they are subjected to a form of "jovial lynching" and condemned to a "solemn and exemplary" punishment. In front of a delirious crowd sitting in the Turin Stadium, the girl will be obliged to have sexual intercourse with three "beautiful, happy, flourishing and Junonic women" who will penetrate her with wooden phalluses, while the boy will be subjected to the violence of three highly gifted men, "among the most handsomely vigorous ones and gifted with the biggest male members in the city".

In Gomorrah, transgression takes place in different ways and implies different punishments: during the screening of a pornographic film in a big open air arena, a middle-aged worker and a young student discover they "are in love" and they start touching each other. "After the first uncertain and terrified moments, the man touches the young student on his thigh, then, little by little, having decided to lose himself in the coitus, he starts touching his genitals. Then he takes the young man's hand and puts it on his member…In a nutshell, the two men 'discover' their identical sexual organs". In accordance with the principles inspired by the most absurd forms of violence and brutality, the two transgressors caught having sex, are insulted and lynched by an angry mob and then condemned to the most severe punishment, "capital execution". The punishment is inflicted in Piazza del Duomo and differentiated for the two "guilty" men: after having been undressed and tortured, the student is pushed into a hole in the ground that is then covered by two marble blocks and is buried alive in front of the Duomo; the worker is instead chained to a helicopter and then killed in the air, so that his blood drips onto the crowd underneath that "(...) shouting and insulting him, receives the blood on their palms and licks it, splashes it on their clothes and faces, in a sort of atrocious ritual of cannibalism".

If, therefore, in Sodom transgressing a prohibition implies an almost bland punishment taking place during an entertaining show based on the law of retaliation, in Gomorrah, the transgression is punished with a macabre orgiastic rite based on the most barbaric violence that calls back to mind the most atrocious executions in *Salò*. Yet the true horror of this Hell that Epifanio and Nunzio discover during their journey, appears only when God casts his revenge against the excesses perpetrated by the two regimes, destroying both the cities and, together with them, their utopias. Despite the peaceful atmosphere in Sodom, after the exemplary punishment of the two heterosexual lovers, some juvenile delinquents try to rape a group of handsome beautiful officials who are sleeping in Lot's house (Lot prefers to offer his wife and three daughters to the city lesbians rather than leaving his guests in the hands of the dangerous sodomites), ending up unleashing the rage of God who throws his punishing lightning bolts on the city, burning it down "like in a surrealist painting" with a terrible fire that quickly turns into a "biblical and apocalyptic scene".

Since the violence and terror ruling Gomorrah is even greater, the destruction of this city takes place in a much more horrifying and gruesome way. God's revenge unravels through a terrible plague that quickly infects everybody, causing "indescribable sufferings", followed by an atrocious death. Citizens are seized by dreadful symptoms: some of them vomit, others develop a "continuous" and severe "diarrhea", and, defecating in the streets, die in their own excrements; other die choking on their own vomit, horrid blotches spread on people's bodies, rotten bulbs fall from the eye sockets, hair falls from people's heads, all the inhabitants of Gomorrah turn into walking corpses covered in festering sores, decomposing little by little, dying one after the other, piling up on immense and horrific heaps.

The third city that the two pilgrims visit along their journey incarnates another utopia, that of socialism. This city is sieged by a fascist army. Numanzia is actually a sort of Paris of the future (even though the atmosphere calls back to mind the Nazi occupation during the Second World War), besieged by a technocratic police that counts, divides and lines up the arriving passengers to send them to concentration camps. While Sodom and Gomorrah were ruled by regimes based on sexual coitus (be it indulgent and homophile, or violent and heterosexual), Numanzia still preserves a certain freedom of expression, that, anyway, under the pressures of the siege, takes its citizens to an extreme solution, that of collective suicide. The poet's proposal, its promotion by the means of communication, the debate in the Parliament, the consequent referendum and the collective decision to commit suicide to avoid fascist enslavement happen during another long sleep that seizes Epifanio, who does not see and therefore takes no part in the crucial moment in which the destiny of an entire city is decided. The end of Numanzia (where each inhabitant chooses the most desirable way to kill himself) is not therefore established by God's revenge that unravels through an apocalyptic cataclysm (a fire, a plague), but it's decided by a human will that plans a sort of "ideological" suicide to prevent a much more atrocious technocratic genocide put into practice by the Neo-Nazi regime.

The arrival of the two travellers in the Orient takes place in an atmosphere of total desolation, in which, little by little, they lose all their luggage and get robbed of their clothes until, after going through landscapes that become more and more unsettling, deserted and apocalyptic, Epifanio is robbed during his final sleep of the precious package that he safely carried in his bosom, containing his gift for the Messiah: a beautiful nativity scene entirely made of gold. The theft of the nativity scene is the beginning of the failure of the very last utopia, represented by the Comet, the utopia of Faith. As the two travellers arrive in their underwear in the fictitious location of Ur, the two discover that the Messiah is not there anymore, or rather that he was born, but he is already dead. Their journey was too long, so long indeed that they arrived "fatally late".

Despite the discouragement and desperation that informs the last part of the script, the conclusion remains mysteriously suspended and unfinished, and the author, rather than closing the text with a hypothetical "ideology of death", does not present the delusion of another utopia, but highlights the acknowledgement of the final revelation that, even though it does not offer any hope, sets the characters onto a new wait. Indeed, from the sky towards which Nunzio (transformed into Angelo) and the spirit of Epifanio (killed by the disappointment) ascended without being able to find any Paradise, the two men observe the Earth, as little as a toy globe, from which everyday voices and noises are coming, followed by revolutionary songs.

In the "silence" and "emptiness" of the sky, Epifanio comments with philosophical detachment: "(...) it was a delusion that led me through the world – but it was that delusion that allowed me to get to know the truth about the world. (...) And yet... as it happened for all the other Comets, also the Comet I followed was a piece of shit. But without that piece of shit, my dear Earth, I would have never got to know you..."

The disenchantment, therefore, produces knowledge and the loss of hope produces the discovery of truth, of reality. If it is true that the utopia comes to an end, it is also true that there is a new waiting process that implies that something may happen, as Nunzio states in the last words that close the script: "The end does not exist. Let's wait. Something will happen." A new beginning? A new "reality"? The possibility of a new mission?

In its surreal and metaphysical dimension the finale fades into ambiguity, leaving maybe the possibility to imagine (also thanks to that distant echo of "revolutionary songs") a future beyond the catastrophe.

2.
PHALLOCRACY, VISIONARINESS AND SARCASM

The text of *Porno-Teo-Kolossal* only exists in its original script-like format, but it features a lot of elements that focus on ideological reflections (with the political and cultural allegories that they imply), the phallocratic idea of sexuality and the game of the "double view" (objective and subjective), directly linked to the last film, *Salò or the 120 Days of Sodom*. In the perfect complementarity of the two cities-utopias based on juxtaposed sexual regimes, it presents a type of vision that highlights male virility and female passivity, favouring the gay relationship over the lesbian one, as established by a strongly phallocratic imaginary (both in a homosexual and heterosexual sense). The "exemplary" punishment the boy and the girl in Sodom are subjected to is based in both the cases on forced penetration: by "Junonic lesbians" with "wooden phalluses" and by "highly gifted young men" with "the biggest male members". The same sudden violence that causes the destruction of the city is exercised by "delinquent sodomites" against a group of young officers, and it's uselessly contrasted by Lot who offers his daughters to the lesbians of Sodom. In the same way, the legalised sexual violence in Gomorrah is an exclusive right of men (above all of initiated young men) upon women who end up being the victims or the accomplices of the system. Similarly, the homosexual passion that triggers a scandal all over the city involves a middle-aged worker and a young student: a couple that somehow reflects in reverse the experiences lived by Pasolini himself, with the intellectual grown-up man surrounded by young men from the *borgate*.

In this triumph of virility exercised in terms of violence (against women) and of passion (only between men), there is only one moment in which female sex is highlighted, albeit in a literal sense, and in an extremely obscene and violent context: during the screening of the pornographic film in the Gomorrah arena. In the script it is indeed specified that during this "very vulgar screening" in which a coitus is represented "in detail", "there is a frame in which the camera seems to be slowly entering, through a pair of perversely spread-eagled legs, a vagina: the latter looks enormous in the giant screen." This image of a vagina is almost monstrous and disgusting, finalised to excite the male audience and prompt it to employ violence in the sexual act.

Also the story of Lot's daughters, inspired by the biblical legend, closes in a grotesque way with a sodomy attempt. After having had sex with their father on the train that is taking them away from Sodom (while being very careful at not turning behind), the girls are attacked as soon as they reach Gomorrah by a group of youngsters who order them to turn "towards South" to sodomise them. As a direct consequence of this act, the girls immediately turn into salt statues, forever frozen into a "ridiculous and indecent posture". The irony applied to the biblical story is clear here: the daughters "get their father drunk and abandon themselves to lascivious acts with him", but in a train carriage, a setting that turns everything into a rather comical scene; in the same way, the curse of the salt statue turns into reality, but on the exact moment they are obliged to turn behind to be sodomised.

Another extremely important characteristic in the script is the "double view" through which different actions in the story intertwine together. The protagonists arriving in the cities and discovering their regimes, the national holidays and the punishments of the transgressors, the apocalyptic scenes and escapes from the plagues are all "subjective", as they are presented from Epifanio's point of view. Together with Nunzio he sees all these things as a silent and helpless, incredulous and frightened witness, without ever taking part in what goes on around him. The only "objective" visions regarding reality, as stated earlier on, are those ones in which Epifanio falls into a "deep sleep" that does not allow him to "see" both the clandestine acts through which the prohibitions are transgressed, and the scandalised reactions followed by the consequent lynching taking place in the two cities. However, there is a moment in which the subjective vision of Epifanio doubles up, becoming at the same time "divided and united", since the scene – and in particular the part of the story regarding the Feast of the Initiation in Gomorrah – is shown first through the "live sequences" broadcast by the television, and then from the point of view of Epifanio who is looking out of the window, to offer a double subjective perspective (the television and Epifanio's) that calls to mind, as Roberto Chiesi underlines, the tortures and executions in *Salò* shown through the binoculars.

The vision of the final horrors in *Salò* was indirect and furtive, but Pasolini, obliging the watcher to spy a voyeur looking at obscene and intolerable acts, made sure that the two points of view overlapped. The same trick was somehow supposed to happen in *Porno-Teo-Kolossal*: the frightening and horrible visions, filtered through the TV screen and impeded by certain obstacles, become even more real and therefore even more vicious. Television assumes the same role of "filter" the binoculars had, selecting the scenes and highlighting the horrors, ending up in offering more realistic than alienating sensations, also thanks to the specifity of the audio visual means that offer a different perspective (more "total" than "personal") compared to the human look.

Even though the text of *Porno-Teo-Kolossal* is extremely rich in hyperreal or rather visionary scenes (as in the vicious and horrible sexual punishments or the apocalyptic destructions), the strong dramatic rhythm of the story is softened by some comical "interludes" courtesy of Eduardo and Ninetto and the recurring figure of the "Neapolitan man" who "helps" the pilgrims in each city. As it happened for the character-masks of Totò and Ninetto, who managed to summon up certain bitter and tormented yet comical moods through their bodies and facial expressions (in particular in *Uccellacci e Uccellini* – "The Hawks and The Sparrows" – and in the ideological-fables), also the complementary characters of Epifanio and Nunzio (a mild and dreamy man versus a brusque and impolite one) create a series of exhilarating situations provoked by the Neapolitan songs sung by Ninetto and by the comical "counter-scenes" mimed by Eduardo, as they travel by train from one city to the next. Apart from these interludes there are also enjoyable meetings characterised by agreements, revelations, confessions and friendly exchanges with the mysterious Neapolitan man who, in his multiple roles of travelling busker in Sodom, weapons dealer in Gomorrah, cook of the Fascist army in Numanzia and driver of the Continental Hotel in Ur, offers protection to the two travellers, revealing himself at the very end as the thief of the precious nativity scene dedicated to the Messiah.

Apart from the typical Neapolitan gestures and expressions that create in different circumstances a rather hilarious atmosphere, there are further tragicomic moments in which grotesque and macabre scenes take place, for example during the celebrations for the occupation of Numanzia. The bizarre quarrel (about the wine brand used for the toast) between the leader of the Fascist army and the poet promoting the collective suicide (the only one who actually won't kill himself), degenerates in the immediate shooting of the latter, who, after betraying his fellow citizens, dies as a hero raising his fist and shouting "Up the Revolution!" for a rather bizarre dispute caused by his stubbornness.

The rhythm of the script underlines not only a "contamination of genres", as stated by Chiesi, but also a "total stylistic contamination", evolving in this way from the "high or dramatic style" of the reality of Sodom to the "sublime and tragic style" of the atrocities of Gomorrah and the "medium or comic style" of the desolation of Numanzia and Ur, finally dissolving in a metaphysical conclusion that leaves any kind of interpretation open. It's not a coincidence that, following a perfectly circular structure, *Porno-Teo-Kolossal* closes with the same initial image of the Earth seen from "the darkness and the silence of the cosmic heights". Yet, while in the opening scenes "the terrestrial globe" was brought into focus little by little, panning on Italy and then on Naples "with its alleys, squares and *bassi* (tiny one-room apartments)" (where the story originated), at the very end "the globe" becomes more distant and blurred, until we can only hear "a confused buzzing of voices" that sparks in the disenchanted Epifanio feelings of "gratitude" and "affection", almost hinting at the fact that the only way to "comprehend" (meaning to understand and embrace) the drama of man – that is the failure of the utopia – is by observing it from a certain distance, from a subjective yet at the same time universal point of view, that may allow us to take in the human struggle ("the voices and noises of everyday life") through a melancholic and disenchanted cosmic look.

Pier Paolo Pasolini (1922–1975)